Book of Plants and Symbols

Anne Dumas

Book of Plants and Symbols

HACHETTE
Illustrated

French
School,
*Garden of
Love*, 15th
century.
Châteaux de
Versailles et
du Trianon.

Contents

*Birth. Sincere
congratulations
on the happy event.*
Postcard, 1925.

Introduction

Because of their beauty or strangeness, their fragility or long life, plants often harbour a hidden meaning which, to venture a personal view, seems just as much a spiritual message. In some places and on certain occasions, the language of plants carries with it thoughts of eternity. It is not unusual for plants to convey the permanence of a memory. Nor is it unusual for them to define the infinite degrees of love, and for certain properties to be linked with them. These meanings, and all the symbols that go with them, date from ancient times when mankind sought to go beyond mere appearances to try and clarify the secrets of Nature, to explain the delicacy of a flower or the incorruptible strength of a tree. The mysteries of such symbolism are often difficult to decode, and can even seem insoluble, because now the cultures and religions of different civilisations are all mixed in together. But in the labyrinthine paths of this mysterious garden you can always feel the tremendous poetry contained in these myths and fables.

The Flowers of Renewal

At the heart of the universal rhythm of the seasons, spring gives us the miraculous spectacle of nature's rebirth. With their delicacy and their scents, flowers make us forget the sorrows of winter. As we rediscover the sweetness of the air, it conveys to us the return of life, its victory over death, and a sense of radiant joy.

The Violet: Humble and Faithful

'Come, Oh gods of Olympus, come and receive the springtime tribute of these violets plaited in rings [...]; for a brilliant feast awaits the poet when the purple-veiled seasons reopen their dwelling, and fragrant spring revives the divine freshness of the plants.'

Pindar

Almost Invisible

Violets are associated with modesty, even timidity. It is true that they are very reserved when, with the first rays of spring sunshine, their little violet and white flowers appear. They have such a habit of hiding away that, if it were not for their delicate scent, they might go quite unnoticed.

And yet the violet (*Viola odorata* L.) does more than conceal itself. It is also the emblem of youth, beauty and generosity.

Classical Fame

Because of its Greek name *Iona*, the Ancients gave the violet a fantastic origin. According to some, Jupiter had it begin life in the meadows where the nymph Io used wander. Jupiter had transformed Io into a cow and had given her pasture to graze in. According to others, the violet grew spontaneously in Ionia and a nymph, seeing this most beautiful of flowers, presented it to the king of the gods.

Be that as it may, the Athenians revered the violet; they decorated their houses with it and the cradles of new-born babies. They also made rings or crowns of violets for their feasts, particularly those in honour of Dionysus, for he had been accorded the virtues of refreshment, suitable for curing headaches caused by drunkenness.

Previous double page:
William Bouguereau,
Spring (detail), 1858. Coll.
Mr and Mrs Harry Glass.

Left:
François Verdier, *The Nymph
Io, Transformed into a Cow,
is Led Away by the Shepherd
Argus, Despite the Pleas of Her
Sisters and Her Father, the River
God Inachus,* 1693. Châteaux
de Versailles et du Trianon.

The Bouquet of Violets

'I always remember the extraordinary effect that a bouquet of violets at Christmas had on me. When I was given them, I was in that serious state of mind you often fall into in the winter months; my imagination was asleep; my thoughts were cold and I could hardly feel anything. Suddenly, the colour of these violets and their delicate scent struck my senses: I was brought back to life. A gentle shiver ran through my limbs, the will to act took hold of me; happy images rushed through my mind, a pinkish colour spread across the horizon of my life; my courage was aroused, and I was able to do so much more.'

Madame Roland de La Platière, letter to Mademoiselle Cannet.

The Princes of the Church took it as their colour, and it was also used to mourn kings.

In Memoriam

'Violets are the smile of the dead,' wrote the poet Paul-Jean Toulet. In fact, this was a very old symbol. The Romans thought violets were the flowers of mourning, of memory and affection for the dead. They decorated tombs with wreaths of violets on the Day of the Dead, known for that reason as the 'Day of Violets' (*Violaris dies*). An echo of this ancient practice probably survives in our use of the colour violet for mourning, penitence and meditation.

The Emperor's Violet

In the Middle Ages, Western countries made the violet the symbol of faithfulness in love. It was made into crowns for the winners of poetry competitions which took place in the era of courtly love. This is why, when the Academy of Toulouse was appointed to become the Academy of the Floral Games, it chose the Toulouse violet as the supreme prize. Then violets arrived in gardens...

In Paris in the 17th century, street-sellers sold bunches of violets which had been picked in the forests near the capital. It was not until the 1750s that horticulturists had the idea of cultivating violets close to Paris. Perhaps Marie Antoinette made this fashionable. Violets were very popular in gardens in the 19th century, and under Napoleon III the flower became the symbol of the regime, in memory of Emperor Napoleon I, who returned from the island of Elba on 1 March, the month of the violet. Its sales and cultivation increased, and new varieties were introduced.

Right:
Sir James Dromgole Linton, *Violets*, 19th century. The Maas Gallery, London. The violet is one of the flowers of the Nice region, where they grow it to make perfume. The most sought-after variety, the Parma violet, has an intoxicating scent.

The Smile of Springtime

Snowdrops and crocuses are the first to show signs that nature is returning to life. They are the first fruits of spring's arrival, and are soon followed by primroses, daisies, violets, pansies and wallflowers. All these flowers are messengers of hope and symbols of a return to gentler times.

The Primrose, an English Favourite

This flower belongs to the genus *Primula*, a name derived from the medieval Latin *primula veris*, literally meaning the 'firstling of spring'. This is the flower that really heralds the beginning of springtime. Its best-known variety is the cowslip, with its yellow flowers. Cultivated primroses, with large flowers, differ from the cowslip in that their calyx bulges out less and they come in various colours. It seems that the Ancients were not aware of the primrose. However that may be, there is a more recent legend about the cowslip which the English are very fond of. During the second half of the 19th century, a ball was given in honour of the Prime Minister, Benjamin Disraeli, at which a young woman was seen wearing a crown of cowslips as her only form of adornment. Her graceful attitude attracted a lot of attention. People started talking about her. Were the flowers natural or artificial? Disraeli himself asked the young woman about her pretty crown, and learned that she had picked the flowers in a nearby meadow. From that time on, the great statesman often wore a cowslip in his buttonhole. In England, too, a Primrose League was formed, and each year on the anniversary of Disraeli's death its members cover his tomb with flowers and decorate his statues with garlands.

A Miniature Marguerite

'I walked with my arms raised to the sky, wanting to pick the stars that fled from me, and did not deign to pick the little daisy which

The daisy, whose Latin name *Bellis perennis* describes it as a perennial, is in French the *pâquerette* or 'flower of Easter', the time it begins flowering.

Drinking Cowslips

'In the north, they make a drink out of cowslips, fresh flowers, water and honey. It is a very sparkling drink because of the large amount of carbonic acid the flower contains; so is the sparkling wine from Hamburg, which looks like Champagne. They eat cowslip leaves in a salad, and mix them in tea to give it a certain aroma.'

Le Journal de la Jeunesse, 1903.

Left:
J.-J. Grandville, 'Primrose and Snowdrop' in *Les Fleurs Animées,* 1847. Bibliothèque Forney, Paris.

Right:
The cuckoo is one of the first birds to announce that spring is here. As soon as it has sung, two yellow flowers burst into flower: the cowslip, shown here, and the daffodil.

Below:
A. H. Payne, after J.-J. Grandville,
The Palace of the Queen of Flowers, 1854.

Opposite:
William Bouguereau, *Spring*, 1858.
Coll. Mr and Mrs Harry Glass.

A.H. Payne sc.

opened its golden heart to me in the dew of the lawn,' wrote Théophile Gautier in his novel *Mademoiselle de Maupin*. Although the meadow daisy may seem quite insignificant, the cultivated varieties of this 'little marguerite' are just as delicate and perfect as their big sister. Proof of this can be seen in the work of late medieval painters, who were very interested in it. After them, at the beginning of the 17th century, Jan Brueghel, also known as Velvet Brueghel, included it in his still lifes. This interest can be explained by the fact that, in popular worship, the daisy, which flowered everywhere, was the symbol of the Virgin Mary, 'of her triumphant love of all things', as Leo Wuyts tells us. This is why, in Flanders, it is still called *madeliefje* or *meizoetje*, names derived from *Maghet lieve* ('beloved Virgin') and *Maghet suete* ('sweet Virgin').

The marguerite can tell you about love. The petals are plucked one by one to the chant: 'He/She loves me, He/She loves me not.'

Under the Sign of Flora

In Ancient Rome, festivals known as the Floralia were held every year in her honour. From the Renaissance onwards, her image as the goddess of flowers was very popular. Probably, too, Fabre d'Eglantine was thinking of her when he called the eighth month of the French Republican calendar Floréal.

Below:
When Rembrandt portrayed his wife Saskia in *Flora* (1634), the painting was full of poetry. Hermitage Museum, St Petersburg.

The 'Mother of Flowers'

That is what Ovid called her. Flora was in fact the goddess of vegetation. In Rome, a temple was dedicated to her on the Quirinal, and another near the Circus Maximus. The true 'personality' of this divinity remains mysterious, two traditions having become intertwined. One concerns the Flora of the Greeks, associated with the nymph Chloris. She was loved by Zephyr, the West Wind, who married her in May; the empire of flowers was her wedding present. The other is the Roman Flora, known by the name *Acca Larentia*, whose Floralia, fairly licentious cultic festivals, suggest that before she became a goddess, she was a courtesan.

Flora's Clock

Flowers tell the time. In the old days, in the countryside, people guessed the time of day by looking at nature, to see whether the flowers had opened or closed their corollas. Pliny put forward the idea that the flowering time of plants could be used to define the different seasons of the year. It seems he even planned to produce a plant

calendar. At all events, this did not happen until the time of Carolus Linnaeus. This Swedish botanist based his Flower Clock on the fact that some plants sleep in a very regular pattern, always falling asleep and waking up at the same time regardless of the season. So he brought together a series of sleeping plants, each of which woke up at a different time. The daytime flowers 'lived' between three o'clock in the morning and two o'clock in the afternoon, while the nocturnal flowers came to life in the period between four o'clock in the afternoon and midnight. Linnaeus's clock was designed to fit the Scandinavian climate, so when the naturalist Lamarck adapted it for France, his clock was a little ahead of the one in Uppsala.

Flora's Barometer

It is interesting to note that some flowers do not have the same regular sleep pattern, but live according to atmospheric conditions, and so can serve as barometers, even hygrometers. At one time, this was a common practice. People observed the marigold, which closed its corolla as soon as the sky became covered with dark clouds heralding rain; the primrose, which behaved in a similar fashion; and the Siberian sow-thistle which, being used to the cold, closed its flowers when the sun shone and the temperature went up... and even the rose, whose scent became stronger when rain was near.

Opposite:
The Swedish naturalist Carolus Linnaeus (1707–1778).

Left:
Giuseppe Arcimboldo, allegorical figure of *Flora*, 1591. Private Collection, Paris.

Flora, from a late 19th-century chromolithograph.

The Gracious 'Narcissus of the Poets'

Its white flower, adorned in the centre with a small red or orange-red cup, is highly scented. The narcissus is a symbol of spring and is also, because it sleeps for a long time and wakes up on fine days, associated with ideas of death and rebirth.

A Famous Myth

Narcissus (*Narkissos in Greek*) was the handsome son of the river-god Cephissus and the nymph Liriope. At his birth, the soothsayer Teiresias predicted that he would have a long life provided he never saw himself. Echo, the daughter of the Air and the Earth, was a nymph of the springs and forests, and fell in love with Narcissus. Echo had been deprived of the power of speech by Hera, and was condemned to repeat only the last words that were spoken to her. She could not manage to attract the attention of Narcissus who, in any case, only showed contempt and indifference to others. So she implored the help of Nemesis, goddess of divine vengeance, who punished Narcissus by making him drink from a pool. Its clear water showed Narcissus his own reflection. He immediately fell in love with it and, unable to take his eyes away from it, took root and was transformed into the elegant flower which bears his name.

Left:
The narcissus, portrayed by Pierre-Joseph Redouté, a specialist botanical artist around the beginning of the 19th century.

Right:
The narcissus in *Les Fleurs Animées* by J.-J. Grandville, 1847. Bibliothèque Forney, Paris.

Opposite:
Nicolas Poussin, *Echo and Narcissus*, 17th century. Musée du Louvre, Paris.

Mysterious Jonquils

The jonquil (*Narcissus jon-quilla*), a variety of narcissus, is so named because its leaves are like those of a rush. Unlike the narcissus of the poets, its flower is bright yellow. It has always been highly prized in China. In the middle of the 19th century, according to the report of a journey by the botanist Robert Fortune, it was common in the streets of Canton to grow bulbs in small receptacles filled with water and white pebbles. The bulbs were inserted upside down, which forced the plants to grow crookedly. In this way the Chinese obtained dwarf and strange-looking jonquils, which they used to decorate houses and temples.

Through the Mirror...

The myth of Narcissus transcends the simple origins of a flower. It is the expression of self-love and 'sublimation to an ideal' (Gaston Bachelard). Paul Valéry describes it poetically:
'But I, beloved Narcissus, am only curious
    About my own essence;
For me, everything else is only a mystery,
    Everything else is only absence.'

A Multiple Symbol

In mythology, the narcissus is also associated with Hell. Proserpine was picking the flower when Pluto, captivated by her beauty, carried her off and took her with him to Hell. This is why some images depict her with a bouquet of narcissi in her hand.
In the flower pictures of the Flemish painters, the narcissus is a symbol of resurrection and also often appears in portrayals of the Virgin, because its shape is quite like that of her flower, the lily.

The narcissus was introduced into China in the Middle Ages and there, known as *shiu-xian*, 'the immortal from the water', it symbolises happiness and is given away with good wishes for the New Year. Finally, in Arab poetry, its stalk represents a man standing or a devoted servant.

Narcissus used as a decorative motif for an ebony cabinet with a Florentine mosaic of hard stones, stamped Joseph Baumhauer, 1765–1770. Château de Versailles et du Trianon.

Opposite top:
Henri Fantin-Latour, *Spring Flowers*, 1869. Private Collection.

Left:
In the manner of Jan Brueghel, *Still Life with Bouquet of Flowers*, 1600. Städelsches Kunstinstitut, Frankfurt. Jan Brueghel was known as 'Velvet Brueghel' or 'Brueghel of the Flowers' because of his liking for flower paintings. He often used narcissi in his compositions, as here, to contribute to the overall harmony.

The Tulip: a Flower of Passion

Although the tulip has no mythological past and has not inspired memorable symbols, it does embody, more than any other flower, the speculative mania that seized plant collectors from the end of the 16th century in their hunt for spectacular varieties.

Oriental Beginnings

Tulips have long been a favourite of painters and poets. They flower during the first half of spring and have a surprising history. The plant's name comes from the Italian *tulipano*, which in turn was derived from the Turkish word *tülbend* (hat or cap), which is also the source for the word 'turban'. The Mogul emperors loved their gardens, and were especially fond of tulips. It seems, though, that they were even more popular in Asia Minor. In Turkey, they were highly prized and thought of as an

Opposite:
Claude Monet, *Tulip Fields in Holland*, 1886. Musée d'Orsay, Paris.

Right:
Félix Vallotton, *Two Pots of Red and Yellow Tulips*, 1916. Private Collection, Switzerland.

ornamental plant with a religious connotation. This is why it was used so much as a decorative motif for both civil and religious buildings.

An Immediate Fascination

The tulip was introduced into Europe in the middle of the 16th century as a result of diplomatic relations with Constantinople. The Dutch rapidly became completely devoted to it. In 1589, the Flemish botanist Charles de l'Ecluse, also known as Carolius Clusius, described nine different varieties imported from Turkey. A few years later, after this bulb collector had moved to the Rhenen area, he accepted the position of director of the botanical garden in Leyden, and made Holland the capital of the tulip.

The Frenzy of the 'Tulip Fanatics'

The tulip trade was established and continued to grow until the 1630s. Unusual and rare plants were prized above all others. Some traders bankrupted themselves for

Beauty and Majesty

'These flowers, more than many others, deserve [...] the most sincere praise and affection of all who love their beauty, both in their majestic appearance and the admirable variety of colours which they reveal every day. [...] But, more than any other flower, tulips can be put together, each colour blending with another and showing it off, so much so that the place they occupy resembles a strange work of embroidery or a painting. I once saw a garden where the owner's skill in arranging his tulips by colour deserved as much praise as the quality of his flowers or anything else.'
John Parkinson,
*Paradisi in sole,
Paradisus terrestris*
(1629).

Pierre-Joseph Redouté, *Cultivated Tulip*, 19th century. The oldest tulip in Europe, used to breed many varieties, was named after the Swiss naturalist Gesner, who introduced it in the middle of the 16th century.

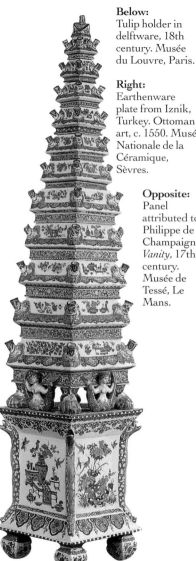

Below:
Tulip holder in delftware, 18th century. Musée du Louvre, Paris.

Right:
Earthenware plate from Iznik, Turkey. Ottoman art, c. 1550. Musée Nationale de la Céramique, Sèvres.

Opposite:
Panel attributed to Philippe de Champaigne, *Vanity*, 17th century. Musée de Tessé, Le Mans.

the sake of an exceptional variety which could be sold for as much as a diamond. For a single bulb, one collector handed over a fine brasserie which for a long time was called the 'Brasserie de la Tulipe'. Between 1634 and 1637, tulip mania reached new peaks in Holland. Nearly five hundred varieties were bought and sold, and the competition was fierce. People gambled on tulips as others did on the Stock Exchange, according to the laws of supply and demand, and often neither the buyer nor the seller had seen the item in question, which was usually just a single bulb.

A Religious Message

Perhaps the tulip symbolises the vanity of the things of this world. A painting by Philippe de Champaigne (17th century) suggests this by featuring a tulip next to a skull and an hour-glass. In the same period, the Jesuit father Alard Le Roy wrote that 'it inflames the soul with the desire to enhance its attractiveness with all kinds of virtues'. In 1644, the Anglican bishop Joseph Hall used it for an 'occasional meditation' and associated it with the marigold. Both these flowers closed their petals each evening, and seemed to him 'Clients of the Sun', their lives depending on its movements. This led him to reflect: 'Such is a good person before God. The choice is entirely ours; our own Sun will bear us away. O God, be for me what you are in yourself; be merciful and take me unto yourself; I shall be happy to follow you.'

Ritual Uses

It is easy to interpret the symbolic values of some flowers and trees through the celebrations in which they were originally involved. The popular taste for myths and the tendency to dream which they convey helped this kind of worship. Some practices have survived to our own times, and although they have lost their 'religious' meaning, they are still valid rituals.

May Day's Good-Luck Flower

In the Renaissance, the lily of the valley was used along with other flowers for garlands. Today, its little white bells are the centre of a modern ritual. Giving a bunch of lily of the valley is said to bring happiness to loved ones.

A Nice Tradition

On the First of May, the month of Flora, there have always been celebrations relating to nature. In Touraine, the custom is to pick hawthorn; in the Morvan, they pick verbena. Some maintain that the lily of the valley tradition associated with this day – the day devoted to the celebration of work – began in the Ile-de-France at the beginning of the 20th century. Some cities, such as Rambouillet, still organise festivals in honour of this flower. Others say it started in Burgundy, where festivities are still dedicated to it. Yet others claim it originated in Celtic culture. However that may be, the practice is nowadays widespread, and everyone in France is aware of it.

A Legendary Perfume

The lily of the valley is also known as the May lily and the Lawn of Parnassus. The latter name comes from the legend in which Apollo created it to cover the ground at Parnassus, where the Muses lived. In French it is the *muguet*, a word derived from the Latin for 'musk' and referring to its smooth, slightly musky scent.

A Thousand and One Beneficial Effects

In the past lily of the valley used to be a medicinal plant. Its flowers were distilled to make a soothing essence known

Previous pages:
Pierre-Charles Trémolières, *Venus and Cupid*, 1738. Musée d'Art et Histoire, Cholet.

Left:
Religious symbolism links the lily of the valley with the humility of the Virgin, the Lord's servant. B. Zeitblom, *Annunciation* (detail), 1497. State Museum of Art, Bucharest.

Opposite:
'The May Day Lily of the Valley', *Le Petit Journal*, 5 May 1907.

The Maytime Tradition

Sometimes a young man put his may tree, decorated with flowers and garlands, on the roof of his girlfriend's house, or even on the chimney; this was somehow meant to show that he had conquered her heart. May trees could also be communal. They were planted in the village square by the young men in honour of the young women they wished to marry. Dances reinforced the magical power of the symbolic tree.

as *eau d'or*, a kind of remedy particularly helpful for irregular heartbeat. In addition, the flowers were dried and ground to make a very popular remedy for a headcold. Another preparation was made by extracting the flower's juice to make an oil. To do this, according to *La Nouvelle Maison Rustique* (1804), you 'fill an airtight container with lily of the valley flowers, then bury it in an ant heap until the flowers turn into juice. It is anodyne, and excellent for gout and herpes.'

The May Tree: an Old Custom

The month of May marks the beginning of spring and has long been a time of feasts and rejoicing. Since the Middle Ages, it has been customary to plant a tree or a large leafy branch and call it the May Tree. Planting a may tree was originally done to honour some high-ranking person. In Paris each year, the law clerks cut down a tree in the Bois de Vincennes and solemnly planted it in the main courtyard of the Palace, which became known as the

May Courtyard. Meanwhile, the city's goldsmiths carried their offering of a may tree to the Cathedral of Notre-Dame. In Lyon, the printers put up a may tree in front of the governor's door and chanted poetic tributes to him.

The tradition was even stronger in the countryside. On the eve of the first of May, young men planted a small leafy tree decorated with ribbons at the their fiancée's door, as a sign that they were engaged. If a tree was missing, it meant the couple had broken up. Some perfumes had a special meaning. Lilac celebrated the beauty of a young woman; elder reproached her for laziness, and holly meant that she had a difficult personality.

Above: Illustration by J. Gazé in *La Gazette du Bon Ton*, May 1914. The may tree, revamped by the world of fashion. Private Collection, Paris.

Opposite above: Dancing round a lime tree, engraving from the *De Stirpium historia* or *Teragus*, 1552. Bibliothèque de l'Ecole de Pharmacie, Paris.

Opposite below: Peasants celebrate May at Gimpelsbrunn, Germany, 1530.

Celebrating Love

*Flowers have always been
used as a sign of love.
The idyllic medieval Gardens
of Love are one of the most
beautiful examples of this.
Flowers were made up
into rings and
bouquets, and sent
to convey passion,
or as a sign
of hope and
fidelity.*

The Carnation: the Flower of Engagements

In France, the red carnation was the emblem of the Royalists. In German countries it was adopted by the Social Democrats, while the white carnation became the flower of the Christian Democrats. As well as its political links, the carnation has a deep religious meaning.
What is more, it has always been seen as the flower of lovers.
'See my pot of carnations / What a lovely bunch / To make bouquets / For lovers!'
That was the cry of the street-seller of carnations who worked the streets of Paris in the 16th century. The flower was associated with betrothal and the notion of lasting love which this required. Paintings from the Middle Ages and the Renaissance show that it was customary to give a symbolic carnation to the loved one at this time. It was apparently also done at weddings, to go with the vow of fidelity.

Orange Flowers for Marriage

Not long ago, it was inconceivable to get married without orange flowers, for the bride's bouquet, often decorated with a knot of white satin, or for a pretty

Bridal outfit (detail).
Bibliothèque Forney, Paris.

Right:
'Jacobeus Claes Trajectensis', known as Jacob Claesz of Utrecht, *Young Woman with a Carnation*, c. 1520. Musée du Louvre, Paris.

Opposite bottom:
Raimundo de Madrazzo y Garreta, *Portrait of Monsieur de Waru*, 1914. Musée d'Orsay, Paris. Fashionable men used to wear a carnation in their buttonhole.

The 'Flower of God'

The carnation, the 'flower of God' (*Dianthus*), was introduced into Europe in about the 12th century, and symbolises the eye of God from which nothing escapes. In addition, whether or not because its narrow leaves suggest nails, it came to embody the Passion and the Crucifixion of Christ. It does not appear in pictorial representations of Christ on the Cross, but in depictions of the Virgin and Child, in which Mary holds a red carnation out to Jesus.

The carnation certainly has a reputation for intensity, and in one of Rembrandt's dark pictures that he painted so expertly, an internalised portrait of *The Woman with a Carnation* (1665–1669), he conveys a spirituality that is one of the flower's essential qualities.

floral crown which she wore in her hair. This is a very old tradition. Zeus is said to have given orange flowers to Hera when he chose her for his wife. Leo Wuyts explained that this flower's symbolic role came from the fact that the tree 'bears leaves, flowers and fruits at the same time. It can therefore be seen variously as an emblem of love and marriage. The leaves are always green, and became the symbol of lifelong love. Its white flowers symbolise the fiancée's sincerity, while the fruits, which ripen between the flowers, represent hope for an heir.'

Carnations by Pierre-Joseph Redouté.

The Rose: Ritual Flower of Beauty and Love

'When, still streaming
with paternal waves,
Aphrodite rose
from the blue sea,
Sparkling naked
in the sunlight,
Jealous Earth
brought forth the rose;
And all of Olympus,
transported by love,
Greeted the flower of Beauty.'
Leconte de Lisle,
Odes Anacréontiques.

Opposite:
School of
Fontainebleau,
Allegory (detail),
c. 1570. Musée
du Louvre, Paris.

The 'Queen of Flowers'

In Ancient times, the rose was dedicated to Aphrodite, goddess of love and beauty. Possibly this exceptional flower came from the Orient. It features regularly in Persian poetry. It is associated with the colour of the beautiful woman who delights the hearts of men. Its pink colour is compared to that of wine, that 'elixir which fortifies the soul' (Omar Khayyam).

The Delicate Crown of Roses

The poets of Antiquity crowned themselves with roses. Cupid, the son of Mars and Venus, is depicted as a child, armed with a bow and quiver, carrying a crown of roses. So, in springtime, is Priapus, the god of gardens and fertility. The use of roses in crowns was continued in the Middle Ages, when the symbolism of flowers grew to include the different forms of love. This is revealed in the allegorical *Roman de la Rose*, by Guillaume de Loris and Jehan de Meung (13th century).

P.-J. Redouté,
Hybrid Bengal
Tea Rose.

The Rose in Religion

In the 12th century, the Church introduced the rose into its ceremonies. People used red roses to make up rosaries, for

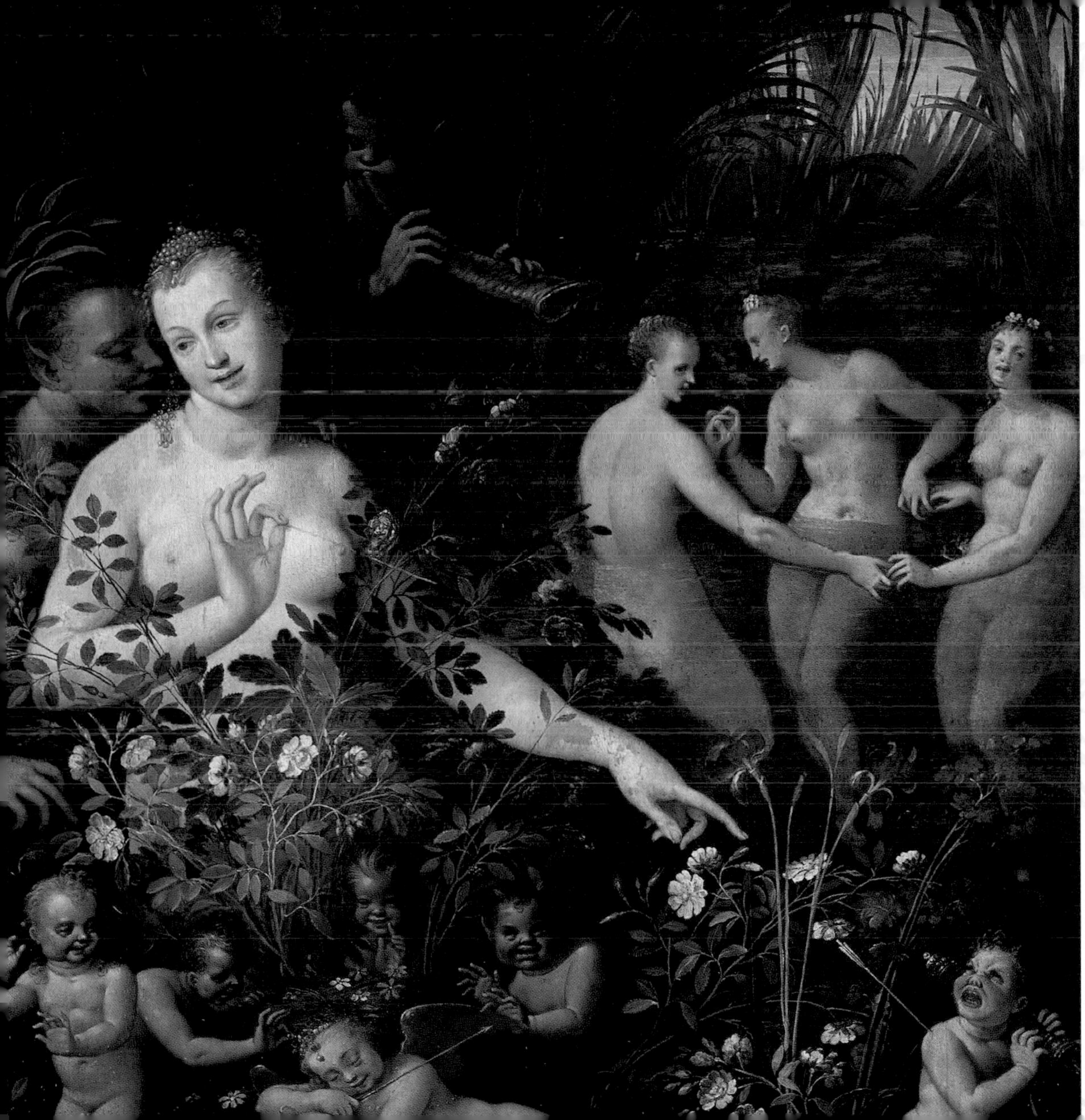

Illumination from a 15th-century manuscript of the *Roman de la Rose*. This medieval work shows a rose tree filled with flowers whose scent hangs heavy over a mysterious garden. British Library, London.

Right:
Golden rose made of gold and enamel by Minuchio Jacobi da Siena, 1330. Musée du Moyen Age-Cluny, Paris.

example. At Whitsun, formerly known in France as 'Rose Easter', probably because it occurred when roses were in flower, processions were showered with rose petals. In Christian symbolism, the white rose represents monastic wisdom, while the red rose stands for the Passion and the blood of Christ.

The Pope's Golden Rose

In the 11th century, under the rule of Popes Leo IX and Urban II, documents show that a massive bouquet of gold roses was solemnly blessed by the Pope on the fourth Sunday of Lent. After the Mass, he carried the bouquet in procession, and then sent it to a Catholic prince or princess. In 1515, Leo X sent the bouquet to Archduke Charles, the future Charles V. From the 18th century, only queens received the Golden Rose. The last to do so, in 1937, was Helen of Savoy, wife of the King of Italy, Victor-Emmanuel III.

Leasing the Roses

This unusual ritual was established in the 14th century. It involved the dukes and peers of France under the jurisdiction of the Parliament in Paris. Three times a year, they had to present a basket of roses to the magistrates of this court. The peer responsible for the ceremony had flowers, mainly roses, strewn round the various chambers of Parliament, organised a lavish lunch and 'then went round each chamber to the sound of harps and flageolets with, borne in front of him, a large silver bowl full of roses' (*Magasin Pittoresque*, 1839). Then the 'lease' was conducted by the peer whose turn it was to take charge of presenting the roses. This custom was taken very seriously by the peers because it fixed their precedence, which had disappeared when Parliament was transferred to Tours following the troubles with the League. The last to take

'An Oriental count said that the rose was made white by God, but Adam was looking at it just as it opened; the rose was ashamed and turned pink.' (Victor Hugo, *Les Misérables*).

Above:
Piero della Francesca, *Madonna de Senigallia* (detail), c. 1470. Galleria Nazionale delle Marche, Urbino.

The Rose

'[...] The Rose is the honour
  of a vow,
The Rose is the most beautiful
  of flowers
And takes the prize above all
  others;
This is why I call it
The violet of Cyprus.
The Rose is the bouquet of Cupid,
The Rose is the play of the
  Charities,
In the morning the Rose
Lights up with tiny drops
Borrowed from the daybreak.
The rose is the perfume
  of the Gods,
The Rose is the honour of virgins,
Who much prefer
To enrich their bosoms
With new Roses
Than with gold, however precious.
Is nothing beautiful without
  them?'

Pierre de Ronsard,
The Continuation of Love.

Right:
Flemish School, *Portrait of Margaret of York*, sister of Edward VI, King of England, whom Charles the Bold, Duke of Burgundy, married in 1458, 15th century. Musée du Louvre, Paris.

The Rosicrucian Symbol

'Who then wed roses
   to the cross?
Their garland swells
   to gently enfold
The rough wood,
   on all sides.
And pale silver clouds,
   like those in the sky
Float over the scene
   bearing cross and roses,
And a holy life springs up
   from their centre
And a triple beam grows
   from a single point.'

Goethe,
The Mysteries.

Above: Apron bearing the Rosicrucian symbol, 19th century. Musée du Grand-Orient de France, Paris.

Opposite: Henry A. Payne, *Choose between the Red and the White*, end 19th century. Birmingham Museum and Art Gallery.

part was Henri III, King of Navarre, in 1586; three years later he was appointed King of France under the name of Henri IV.

The Rose and Politics

The rose has long been used as a political device. In England in the 15th century, there was an implacable dynastic conflict between two branches of the Plantagenet family disputing the throne. Both had a rose as their emblem, only the colour was different: red for the Lancasters, white for the Yorks. The bitter Wars of the Roses, which broke out in 1450 during the reign of Henry VI, was a bloody fight which shook the monarchy. It was only resolved when, in 1485, Henry Tudor, Duke of Richmond, took the throne as Henry VII. He was descended via his mother from the House of Lancaster, and allied to the House of York by his marriage to Elizabeth of York.

A Bouquet of Feelings:
the Garland of Julie

*P**oetry is honoured with crowns and garlands of flowers. Its muse, the nymph Erato, was herself crowned with myrtle and roses. A mass of allegorical tributes sang of real, imaginary and impossible loves.*

Below:
Christine de Pisan presenting her book to Elisabeth of Bavaria. Illustration from the *Complete Works* of Christine de Pisan. British Library, London.

Portrait of Charles de Saint-Maure, duc de Montausier par L'Armessin. Bibl. Nat., Paris.

A Garland of Flowers and Love

Although the poets of the Middle Ages excelled at love poetry, its real Golden Age came in the 17th century, when refined courtiers made it their favourite method of expression. In the spring of 1634, Marquis Charles de Montausier, who was appointed a duke in 1665 and governor of the Grand Dauphin in 1668, paid poetic homage to Julie d'Angennes, daughter of the Marquise de Rambouillet, whom he was in love with for 14 years before, marrying in 1645. He presented her with *The Garland of Julie*, the most famous of the allegorical tributes, which he and others wrote to his specifications.

'Receive, O adorable nymph,
Who rules over men's hearts,
This crown more lasting
Than those placed
On the heads of kings.
The flowers I composed with
Put to shame those golden
Flowers in the firmament;
Watered by Parnassus
They are so fresh
They will last forever,

And every day my beautiful Flora,
Who loves me and whom I adore,
Reproaches me with ire
Because my sighs, for her,
Never yield a flower so lovely
As I have composed for you.'
This was how the marquis, identifying himself with Zephyr, addressed his loving anthology to Julie.

A Unique Work

Many of the great wits of the day wrote parts of this lover's offering. They were all regular visitors to the Hôtel de Rambouillet and friends of the marquis. The collection consisted of 29 sheets of vellum, bound by Le Gascon in red Morocco leather and protected by a perfumed case. Each sheet included a flower, painted by Nicolas Robert (1614–1685), beside a poem or poems relating to it. They were inscribed by the calligrapher Nicolas Jarry. In total, there were 62 poems, dedicated to the rose, the narcissus, the lily, the violet, the marigold, the poppy, the orange flower, the anemone, the angelica, etc. The authors included Chapelain, Racan, Madame de Scudéry (sister-in-law of Madeleine de Scudéry), Claude Maleville, Tallement des Réaux, Desmarets de Saint-Sorlin and the marquis himself, who wrote 16 pieces.

Abraham Mignon, *Flowers on a Display of Fruit*, 1660. Gemäldegalerie, Dresden.

Bottom left: Balthazar Peruzzi, *Apollo and the Nine Muses*. Palazzo Pitti, Florence.

The Lily

Before you I lose the victory
That my pallor gave me,
And claim no other glory
Than to hand you the crown.

Heaven, in its great goodness,
Once chose me alone
As the flower the most worthy
To be presented to our kings.

But if I obtained my request,
My fate would be more glorious
Adorning your head
Than fallen from the skies.

Tallement des Réaux

Holly and Mistletoe: Festive Flowers

'But the universal remedy, the panacea, as the Druids called it, was the famous mistletoe. They thought it was placed on the oak tree by a divine hand, and in the union of their sacred tree and the evergreen mistletoe they saw a living symbol of the doctrine of immortality.'

Jules Michelet,
History of France.

Hansi, *Druid Festival in Alsace*, c. 1915.
Bibl. des Arts Décoratifs, Paris.

The Celtic Rite of the 'Mother Night'

The oak mistletoe was very rare, so the Druids thought it was a plant blessed by the gods. As Pliny recounts in his *Natural History*, on the sixth day of the moon after the winter solstice, they prepared a sacrifice beneath an oak tree bearing the precious plant: two young white bulls were tied to the trunk of the tree. A Druid, dressed in a white robe, pulled the parasitical plant off the tree with the help of a golden sickle. The officiants gathered it in a cloth of white wool, for it was not allowed to touch the ground or it would lose its magic power. The sacrifice followed, accompanied by prayers to the gods.

Mistletoe infused in very pure water made a drink 'which cured everything', enabling the sufferer to fight physical pains and be protected against spells and attempts to poison him, and to make sterile animals fertile – probably because the sticky material in the plant's berries was absorbed in the animals' sperm.

Lively Traditions

The deference accorded by the Druids to mistletoe continued in the countryside for centuries by means of the *guilaneu* (meaning 'New Year mistletoe') – celebrations in which children went from door to door in search of seasonal presents. Ceremonies stemming from Druidic sources were banned by the Church in 1595, and again in 1666.

Nevertheless, for a long time it was the custom in certain areas to hang mistletoe round the necks of children to protect them

Holly, with its dark-green leaves and little red berries, is very popular for decorating houses at Christmas.

Right:
'The Two Sillies' in *La Gazette du Bon Ton*, January 1914. Private Collection, Paris. Illustration by A.E. Marty, inspired by the mistletoe (*Viscum album*), symbol of vitality, beneath which it is customary to exchange kisses on the stroke of midnight on New Year's Eve.

Holly: Useful and Beneficial

Holly (*Ilex aquifolium*) is also one of the main symbols of end-of-year feasts. Its very straight branches of solid and very supple wood have long been used to make punishment rods, whip handles and broomsticks. Its bark was used to make glue. Few, however, still remember the virtues that our ancestors attributed to it. Dried and powdered leaves, and fresh leaves were boiled in water to protect against attacks of fever. Leaves boiled in beer made the drinker sweat and protected him against rheumatism and gout. The fruits were macerated in water, and were sought after as purgatives.

against evil spirits, and to make strings of it to guard against epilepsy and convulsions. The mistletoe was called the 'wood of the Holy Cross' because of its many curative qualities.

The Emblem of Childhood

The Christmas tree links past and present, arousing memories of childhood, glorious moments of the year about to end, and family reunions. The custom started in Alsace where, originally, Christmas Eve was dedicated to Adam and Eve, and a fir tree was erected symbolising the tree of transgression. From the beginning of the 17th century, this evergreen tree, which since Antiquity had been endowed with beneficial properties, became a festive element in itself, and was decorated with hosts, symbols

Top:
Coudouze, *Decorating the Christmas Tree*, 1872. Bibl. des Arts Décoratifs, Paris. After 1650, the Christmas tree reached Germany where it had various names: *Tannenbaum* (fir tree), *Weihnachtsbaum* (Christmas tree), *Christbaum* (Christ's tree) and *Lichterbaum* (tree of lights), for in the 18th century it was decorated with lit candles, symbolising Christ.

of Christ, and apples and paper roses, recalling the Jesse tree, sweets and other things.

The Christmas tree was introduced to Paris in 1837 on the initiative of the German Princess Helen of Mecklenburg, the granddaughter of Louis-Philippe. At the same time it was imported into England. Some maintain that it was German merchants, others that it was Prince Albert who, when he married Queen Victoria, wanted to bring this tradition from his childhood to the English court. On the other hand, it was not until the second half of the 19th century that the United States adopted the Christmas tree, when German immigrants in Pennsylvania introduced it.

Above:
A Christmas Eve party with a fashion slant in *Art-Goût-Beauté*, 1923. Bibliothèque des Arts Décoratifs, Paris. In parallel with the spread of Christmas customs, the decoration of the Christmas tree became more profane, linked more to presents for the children. The Christian celebration was neglected in favour of pleasures of the moment.

'Political' Trees

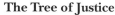

History is full of majestic trees in the shade of which transactions were negotiated, important events planned, and decisions taken about the future of the city. Some continue to be the heart and centre of village communities.

The Tree of Justice

Courts of justice were often held under trees on an appointed day. Popular imagery has perpetuated the memory of audiences given by Saint-Louis beneath an oak tree in Vincennes. Joinville wrote: 'After he had heard Mass in summer, he went and sat beneath an oak tree, and bade us sit near him, and all those who had business with him came and spoke to him without any usher or anyone preventing him.' In this way, in the presence of his entourage and qualified lawyers, the king pronounced his judgments.

The Meeting Tree

In every age, a tree was often the departure point for military missions, resistance movements and misdeeds committed by organised gangs. Beneath a tree people swore faith and allegiance, and took oaths of brotherhood. Because their position

Above:
Next to Fricka is Freya in Wagner's *Rheingold*, 1889. Coll. AKG, Berlin. The lime tree, dedicated in German mythology to the goddess Freya, was the emblem of local law courts. It has always been an important village tree.

enabled people to keep an eye on the horizon, and their thick foliage prevented them from being spied on, and the hollows made in their trunks by time offered hiding places as safe as caves, some trees became places to meet and rally, and even retreat to, and had a historic destiny.

Opposite below:
French School, *Fête on the Place de l'Orme in Paris*, 16th century. Musée Carnavalet, Paris.

Above:
Planting a Tree of Liberty in Paris, 1848. Musée Carnavalet, Paris.

The Tree of Liberty

At the time of the French Revolution, a Tree of Liberty planted in a public square symbolised emancipation and was regarded as a monument. Oak and poplar were the favoured trees, the former because of its Gallic associations, the latter for its evocative Latin name, *Populus*. This tradition was begun in Laon on 1 May 1790, and spread rapidly. In 1791, eighty-five thousand trees had been planted in French territories. The king himself is said to have planted a tree in the Tuileries Gardens that was later ripped out because it was 'withered by despotism'. But most of the trees died, the Revolutionaries casting the blame for this on their enemies. The Convention passed laws to protect them. Nevertheless, very few remained by the beginning of the 19th century.

Liberty and Courage

Today, because of Picasso's great painting, the story of Guernica is more closely linked to the terrible bombardment which destroyed the Spanish town in 1937 than to the ancient oak tree, in the shade of which the old political capital of Vizcaya summoned its Popular Assembly. King Ferdinand II the Catholic and the lords of Vizcaya also swore to keep faith with the ancient charters (*fueros*) under this same tree. Interestingly, the tree perpetuated itself. In the course of time, new shoots took over from the old tree, so maintaining its ancient privileges.

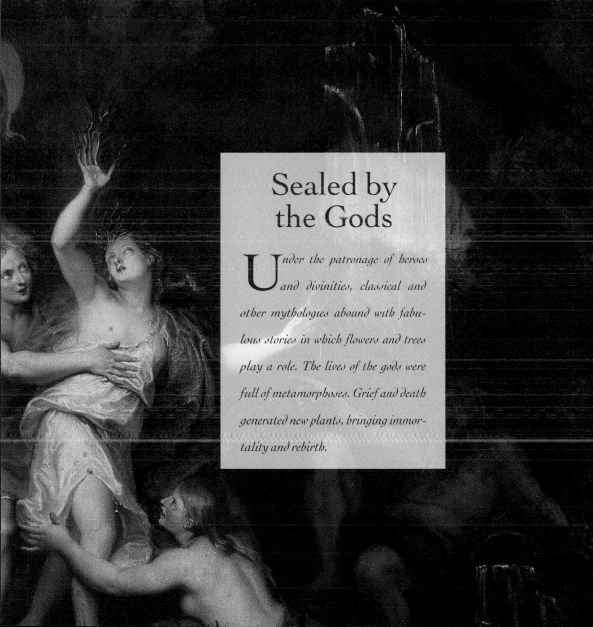

Sealed by the Gods

Under the patronage of heroes and divinities, classical and other mythologies abound with fabulous stories in which flowers and trees play a role. The lives of the gods were full of metamorphoses. Grief and death generated new plants, bringing immortality and rebirth.

Death and Rebirth

'The Ancients did not give up the gifts and promises of the earth to build unapproachable temples. [...] Several demigods and genii were born with a wound and, fertilising the soil with their blood, made a beautiful or medicinal plant spring up.'
Jean de Boschère

The Golden Age of the Hyacinth

The *Hyacinthus orientalis* comes from the Eastern Mediterranean and only had simple flowers when it was introduced to Europe. The Dutchman Pieter Voorhelm of Haarlem improved it around 1680 by giving it double flowers. From then on, it became as much of a craze among collectors as the tulip also was in the same period.

Under Apollo's Protection

The hyacinth is a bulbous plant which produces clusters of flowers and has a penetrating perfume. It owes its origins to Apollo's love for a beautiful Laconian hero called Hyacinthus, the son of Amyclas. The god was practising throwing the discus with the beautiful youth when the discus struck the latter on the head. The west wind Zephyrus – or perhaps the north wind Boreas – were also in love with Hyacinthus, and perhaps in their jealousy diverted the discus from its path. Or perhaps the discus ricocheted accidentally off a rock. This legendary drama remains cloaked in mystery. But little matter! The main thing is that Apollo, mad with grief at having killed his friend, immortalised him by ordering a flower to spring from the blood of the wound, which then took the young man's name.

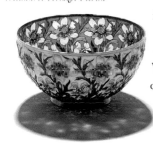

The Grief of Venus

The anemone also sprang from the blood of a
god. Venus was in love with Adonis, the son of
Cinyras, king of Byblos, and his daughter
Myrrha. This passion was to make her despise
the love of the gods. One day when the young
man was out hunting, the jealous Mars turned
himself into a wild boar and wounded Adonis
in the thigh, killing him. Another version
claims that Diana was responsible for the
wild boar's attack, to take her revenge on
Venus who was responsible for the death
of Hippolytus. Whatever the case, Venus
in her despair made a spring flower grow
from the blood of Adonis: the anemone
(from the Greek *anemos*, 'the flower that
opens in the wind'). Also from the drops of his
blood sprang pheasant's eyes (of the genus *Adonis*) with vividly
coloured flowers, one of the best-known being the pheasant's
eye pink. Finally, according to the legend, the goddess herself
was at that same tragic moment wounded in the foot by a
thorn, and the white rose was stained red: thus the red rose
came into being.

An Oracle of Love

The Ancients used anemone leaves for divinatory purposes.
The process was known to Pollux (2nd century AD) who
described it thus: 'You take a poppy or anemone leaf, place
it on the thumb and index finger of the left hand, which are
bent to form a circle, and strike it with the hollow of the right
hand. If the leaf reacts by making a resonant sound, then you
can hope your love will be returned.'

Flowers of the Goddesses

In despair at being abandoned by Apollo, who preferred her sister Leucothoe, Clytia turned herself into a heliotrope. The alder tree was born from the tears of Helen... Many plants have mythological origins, and many flowers derive from the imaginary pantheons of the Greeks and Romans. In its interpretations of these remote references, Christian symbolism has often added its own mark.

The Iris: a Complex Flower

The flower which appears on the arms of France may be an iris, and not a lily as has long been thought. Its name is that of a goddess in the Greek pantheon, Iris, daughter of Thaumas and Electra, a messenger of the gods. When she travelled through the air, as some maintain, or carried her caduceus, as others put it, a surprising phenomenon appeared – a rainbow (*iris* in Greek) – from which the flower takes its array of soft colours and shades.

In the Christian View

According to texts and representations, the iris symbolises the purity of Mary (like the lily and the columbine), with her divine maternity and also, because of her sword-shaped leaves, her grief over the Passion of Jesus. The iris also symbolises the Incarnation of Christ. Its blue colour conveys the innocence of virgins and martyrs, and their faith in Jesus. This symbolism was used in particular by painters of the 14th and 15th centuries.

Hence the iris that appears in *Original Sin* (1467–1468) by the Flemish artist Hugo Van der Goes, and in *The Adoration of the Shepherds* (1476–1478) from the *Portinari Triptych*, painted by the same man.

Opposite:
Baron Pierre-Narcisse Guérin, *Iris and Morpheus*, 1811. This painting was designed as a pendant to *Aurora and Cephalus*. Hermitage Museum, St Petersburg.

P.-J. Redouté, *Iris xiphium*. In the Middle Ages, the iris bore the Latin name *gladiolus*.

The Flower of the Sabbath

Unlike the symbols just referred to, the stinking iris, also known as the 'gladdon', had a bad reputation in the Middle Ages. Its rampant and thick root, with its acrid and irritating taste, made it suitable for the evil spells of witchcraft. It was used, so they say, to make up the ointment that people always rubbed on before the sabbath.

A Royal Legend

'Clovis, on the eve of the Battle of Vouillé, where he defeated the Visigoths, found his advance halted by the River Vienne. A doe, frightened by the clattering of the men's arms, fled and crossed the river without difficulty, at the spot now known as the *Gué de la Biche* (Doe's Ford), not far from Châtelleraut. Yellow iris grew thickly there, and Clovis, full of gratitude and seeking a token of success, picked one of the irises. After he had won the battle, the king of France took the iris as his emblem, and it was also adopted by his successors.

Jacques Brosse,
La Magie des Plantes.

The Mysterious Poppy

The poppy was one of the plants whose leaves were used to divine the future. Its heady, rather acrid scent heralds that of opium smoke, and it is indeed linked chiefly, in most people's minds, to this substance, made from the milky juice of its fruit. Beyond the intoxicated state it produces, which some people have always enjoyed feeling and which we know about from, notably, the dreamlike revelations of Thomas de Quincey (*Confessions of an English Opium Eater*, 1821), opium is principally a valuable medical aid. The products made from it help to deaden pain and calm people's suffering when medicaments no longer have much effect.

Right:
J.-J. Grandville, 'The Poppy' in *Les Fleurs Animées*, 1847. Its pod contains so many small seeds that the poppy is also a symbol of fertility in marriage.

The Poppy: Flower of Oblivion

Like the dittany, the poppy was dedicated to Juno. Because it grew among corn, it was, along with the cornsheaf, an attribute of Demeter (Ceres). This can be explained by the fact that Jupiter had made the goddess inhale it to make her sleep and calm her grief. 'The poppy offered to Demeter symbolises the earth, but also represents the power of sleep and oblivion which overcomes men after death and before rebirth,' explained Victor Magnien in *The Mysteries of Eleusis*. Its sedative and analgesic properties were put to good use by the Ancients, particularly the Egyptians. In the Middle Ages, people were more reticent towards it. Nevertheless, witches used poppy juice, mixed with the grated root of the gladiolus, to make the ointment that induced a hypnotic state and the sensation of mounting a broomstick and flying through the air.

Above:
P.-J. Redouté, *Poppy*.

Opposite:
Giulio Pippi, *Ceres*, Gobelins tapestry, end 17th century. Château de Pau.

The Oak: Father of All Trees

The Latins thought the oak's great size and long life made it the king of all the plants of Europe. With its majestic bearing, it is the symbol of serene power.

Above: Jean-Baptiste Oudry, 'The Oak and the Reed', *The Fables* of La Fontaine, 1729–1734.

Opposite: *Saint Boniface, the missionary from Germany, fells the sacred tree* (724), c. 1900. Westfälisches Schulmuseum, Dortmund.

The Tree of Zeus

The oak symbolises immortality because of the exceptional hardness of its wood. It also represents power, strength and wisdom. The Gallic Druids made it their sacred tree (their own name, moreover, comes from the Greek *drus*, meaning 'oak'). Long before them, however, the Ancients had made it an object of worship, dedicating it to the leader of the gods, Zeus, who had grown up amid the oak forests of Mount Ida. Like the Greeks, the Romans dedicated the oak to Jupiter.

The Tree in the Storm

Oak trees were often struck by lightning, so it was only natural that they should be dedicated to the god of the skies and lightning, in other words Zeus (Jupiter). Among the Scandinavians, the tree was associated with the god of thunder, Thor, son of Odin. Similarly, in other mythologies, the god of thunder also rules the oak; the Russians call him Perun, and the Lithuanians Perkunas.

An Honorary Crown

In the age of myths, it was customary to crown the statues of the gods, both as a solemn avowal of their importance and to solicit their favours. The crown of oak leaves was the attribute of Zeus (Jupiter). When this crown was awarded to a living person, it was done so as a reward. It was given to soldiers for their great deeds in combat and to victorious athletes at the Nemean Games, held in Argolis in honour of Heracles (Hercules). This custom is continued, after a fashion, in France with the decoration for services to education made of two intertwined branches of oak.

René Boivin, *Dance of the Dryads*, 16th century. History is full of legendary oak trees.

Above: Jacopo Ligozzi, botanical plate, 1577–1591. Cabinet of Drawings and Prints, Florence.

The Oracle of Ancient Dodona

According to Herodotus, 'Two black doves flew from Thebes to Egypt. One then flew on to Libya, the other to Dodona. The latter, perching on an oak tree, began to speak in a human voice, saying that an oracle of Zeus should be established at this place. The people of Dodona thought this was an order from the gods and so they founded the oracle.' All the heroes of Greek mythology went to consult the oracle at Dodona. In the *Odyssey*, Ulysses goes there to ask the oracle about his return to Ithaca. Until 219 BC, the year the Temple of Zeus was destroyed by the Aetolians and the site at Epidaurus went into decline, the oracle enjoyed a considerable following, greater even than Pythia's at Delphi. Divine wishes were revealed in various ways, particularly through the rustling of leaves stirred by the wind.

Life Beneath the Bark

Wood nymphs were identified with oak trees and lived beneath their bark. The Dryads could outlive the trees they protected, while the Hamadryads (from the Greek *hamadruas*, literally 'who forms one body with the oak') lived and died with them. The latter nevertheless lived for an extremely long time. Indeed, as Jacques Brosse wrote, 'The life of the oak tree was so long that the Ancients said the Hamadryads lived for 932,120 years.' It was strictly forbidden, under pain of death, to fell these giants of the forest. Every cut had to be made with the priests' authorisation, giving the Dryads time to evacuate the tree.

Russian icon, 19th century, showing the *Oak of Mamre*. This gigantic green oak near Hebron sheltered Abraham when he went there to pitch his tents. Private Collection, Frankfurt.

Above right:
Italian miniature, School of Lombardy or Verona, 'Acorns', illustration from the *Tacuinum sanitatis in medicina*, 14th century. Nat. Library, Vienna.

A Well-meaning Colossus

This powerful and virtuous tree, which the Greeks and Roman believed had provided man's first nourishment, could only be well meaning. Our ancestors used its bark, its acorns and its leaves for various therapeutic purposes, some quite surprising. In 1804, *La Nouvelle Maison Rustique* stated that when the acorn was ground to a fine powder, it was 'astringent, suitable for soothing windy colic', and that 'the Flemish swallowed it in wine to cure the colics that beer gave them'. Even the oak mushroom (*fungus*) was said to be beneficial, like the moss and mistletoe which grew on the tree.

Sacred Trees

*W*oods and forests were the first places to be dedicated to the gods. In the shade of these great trees, the Ancients worshipped their divinities. They also surrounded their sanctuaries with them, believing that they were part of the structure of the world. In some mythologies they were seen as the Pillars of the Universe. Others saw in them the primordial tree from which the human race was born.

Above:
The mysterious ash tree Yggdrasil, tree of the world and tree of destiny, c. 1880. Coll. AKG, Berlin.

The goddess of trees provides the dead with the Water of Life. Tomb of Kha, Egypt. 18th Dynasty. Egyptian Museum, Turin.

The Cosmic Tree

The Tree of the World is to be found everywhere in Ancient beliefs, forming a bond between the dark land of the dead, the earthly world of men and the celestial seat of the gods. Many temples were built to symbolise it. In Sumeria, in the 2nd millennium BC, it joined Heaven and Earth; its roots were sunk in the *apsou*, the 'primordial abyss'. It was called *kiskanu* in Mesopotamia, and is often represented by a fig tree; it is also the residence of the goddess Bau and her son, the god of agriculture and fertility. In Nordic mythology, the indestructible evergreen ash tree Yggdrasil ('Steed of the Redoubtable One' [Odin]) supports the world. One of its roots drew water from a fountain watched over by the Norns, who presided over the fate of humans, and it was also regarded as the 'tree of destiny'. In Chinese cosmogony, *Kien-mou* ('the upright wood') at the centre of the Universe was the tree of the beginning of the world. On either side of it, two gigantic trees were associated with the path of the Sun. One version of the myth emphasises the tree representing the dawn, a hollow mulberry tree, the residence of the mother of the

Suns, a sacred tree symbolising the cosmic order. This symbolism recurs in other civilisations (among the Maya of Mexico, in particular), and makes the tree an example for mankind of wisdom and serenity.

The Trees of Creation

In *Genesis* we read: 'And out of the ground made the LORD God to grow every tree that is pleasant to the sight, and good for food; the tree of life also in the midst of the garden, and the tree of knowledge of good and

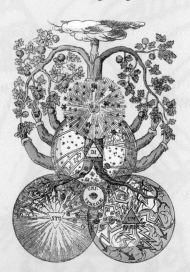

evil. [...] And the LORD God commanded the man, saying, "Of every tree of the garden thou mayest freely eat; but the tree of the knowledge of good and evil, thou shalt not eat of it, for in the day that thou eatest thereof thou shalt surely die."' Breaking this ban deprived man of his innocence. The fruit of the tree of life would have assured man of immortality, but God did not want this, so he banished man from the Garden of Eden and had the tree of life guarded by Cherubims. According to Hans Biedermann, 'The Cross of Christ was constructed from the wood of the "tree of knowledge" of paradise, and so for believers the cross itself became the tree of life.'

A Common Symbol

In many myths the tree of life, unlike the one in *Genesis*, is generally inaccessible. As Jacques Brosse shows, the theme of the Triad constantly

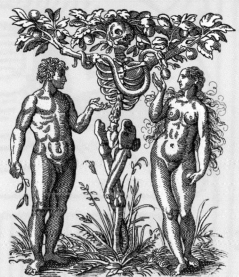

E.H. Langlois, *Adam and Eve Before the Tree of the Knowledge of Good and Evil*, 1883.

Left:
The Tree of the Knowledge of Good and Evil. Rosicrucian allegory, 16th–17th centuries. Germany, new edition, 1785. Bibl. Nat., Cabinet des Imprimés, Paris.

recurs. It features 'the first man or the hero searching for immortality, the tree of life which can give it to him, and the serpent which forbids access to it.' The conclusion is always the same: 'Immortality cannot be acquired except at the price of superhuman trials.'

The Lotus: Almost Divine

'In the middle of the
courtyard, a pool, edged in
granite from Syene, sparkled
in the sun, and on its surface
lay the large heart-shaped
leaves of a lotus, whose
pink and blue flowers were
half-closed, as though
swooning in the heat,
despite the water in
which they bathed.'

Théophile Gautier

Lotus ring, Egyptian
jewel. Musée du
Louvre, Paris.

An Ancient Confusion

In the *Odyssey*, Homer described the companions of Ulysses as so seduced by the sweet lotus which the Lotophagi gave them to eat that they forgot about their homeland. This fruit, with its magical properties, came from a plant on the African coast – probably the jujube lotus – and had no connection with the majestic plant that we now think of. Curiously, the word *lotus*, which is the generic name for the bird's foot trefoil, can also describe plants that have nothing to do with them. But these were the plants which served as a vehicle for myths and legends. This explains the poetic blur in which the accounts of the Ancients lost their way.

A Sacred Aquatic Plant

The lotus that the Ancient Egyptians saw as supporting the sun, derived from the basic alluvium when the world was created, is in fact a water lily. It has a sparkling whiteness (*Nymphaea lotus*) and symbolises purity, but it can also be blue (*Nymphaea caerulea*). The latter is rarer and exceptionally fragrant, and is the attribute of Nefertum, one of the gods of the triad of Memphis, the 'lord of perfumes'. The lotus appeared frequently in the art of Memphis at its peak – in architectural motifs and lotus-shaped columns – and was almost the emblem of Upper Egypt. When Herodotus compared the flower of the Egyptian lotus to that of the lily, he called it the 'lily of the Nile'. On the other hand, Athene called it a 'lotus', so adding to the confusion.

Opposite: Tomb of Cheti, Beni Hassan, c. 1950 BC. The lotus-shaped capital of the column depicts the flower in bud.

Opposite above right: Tomb of Nebamun, west of Thebes. The wife of the deceased holds a bouquet of lotuses, 18th Dynasty. British Library, London.

'Bread' of the Nile

'The Egyptians who live in marshy places use the following means to feed themselves. When the Nile is full and the fields are submerged, an immense number of plants appear on the surface of the water which look like lilies, and which they call *lotos*: the Egyptians cut them and dry them in the sun; then they make a kind of bread from the seeds of this flower, which look like poppy seeds; they also eat the root, which is round and as big as an apple, and has a pleasant perfume.'

Herodotus

Indian miniature, Udaipur, Rajasthan, 17th century. The lotus plays a great part in Indian symbolism. The sacred city of Benares is also known as 'the lotus of the world'. Government Museum, Udaipur.

Opposite above: Akashagarba, goddess of goodness and wisdom. After a 9th-century work, ill. in *The Kokka*, Japan, August 1903. Bibl. des Arts Décoratifs, Paris.

Knowledge and Spirituality

In India, the white and pink lotus (*Nelumbium nucifera* and *Nelumbium nelumbo*) are also associated with the creation. Brahman iconography shows Brahma, the Creator, father of the gods and man, endowed with four arms and four faces, reciting the *Veda*. He is seated, in the middle of a sea of milk, on a pink lotus whose stem, sprouting from the navel of Vishnu, points towards the sky. His wife, Sarasvati, goddess of wisdom, knowledge and music, is also sometimes represented seated on a lotus, while Lakshmi, the wife of Vishnu, was herself born from a lotus growing on the forehead of her husband. Buddhism also gives the plant an important role. At the moment Buddha was conceived, miracles took place and pools were covered in lotuses. The golden lotus, on which the Buddha Gautama often sits, is the attribute of his spiritual omnipotence.

Aspiring to Purity

The lotus also adorns the quiet waters of Chinese gardens and has been honoured there for a very long time. Its large pink flowers, with their strong perfumes, symbolise perfection. 'It emerges from the bowl, but is not contaminated by it; it rests nobly on the clear water [...]. With its radiant purity, The Lotus is to be contemplated from afar and should not be defiled by too direct a contact' (Chu Tun-ju, 12th century). Various symbols are attached to this notion of purity: 'Firmness (the rigidity of the stem), prosperity (the plant's luxuriousness), many descendants (its abundance of seeds), conjugal harmony (two flowers growing on the same stem), and time past, present and future (the three successive states of the plant are visible at the same time: seeds, bud and open flower)' (Pierre Grison).

Seated Buddha, Anuradhapura, Sri Lanka, between 850 and 750 BC.

The Japanese Lotus

In Japan, too, divinities are shown seated on a lotus flower – particularly Quanwon, the goddess of nature, who has 16 arms. Japanese Buddhist painting has many fine compositions of this kind, including those at the pagoda of Daigo-ji, built near Kyoto in 951. The sacred image is inseparable from the beauty of the flower.

The Laurel: Honour and Triumph

The nymph Daphne, daughter of the Thessalian river god Peneius, fled to the mountains to escape the attentions of Apollo. As the god was about to catch her, she pleaded for help from her father, who turned her into a laurel. Apollo endowed the shrub with immortality, and since then it has been dedicated to him.

Below:
Dante Alighieri, by Stefano Tofanelli after Raphael. The laurel was long used to crown poets and writers, also deserving students. The term 'laureate', from the Latin *laureatus*, 'crowned with laurel', is still occasionally used to describe someone who has won a prize in a competition.

Daphne's Magic Powers

The laurel was associated with the cult of Apollo, the keeper of the gift of oracles, and was endowed with divinatory powers. Before Pythia delivered oracles at Delphi, she chewed some of this sacred plant's leaves to put herself in an ecstatic state. Some soothsayers foretold the future by watching a laurel burn after they had set it on fire. It was thought the laurel looked favourably on prophetic dreams, so a branch was placed near the head of a sleeping person to bring this phenomenon into play.

René-Antoine Houasse, *Apollo Pursuing Daphne*. Châteaux de Versailles et du Trianon.

Emblem of Glory and Merit

The Ancients made crowns from laurel leaves for their heroes and others famed for their wisdom or special talent. The laurel was seen as the symbol of victory, over others or oneself, and of the peace which resulted. In Ancient Rome, a general honoured by a triumph held a laurel branch in his left hand. The Senate awarded Julius Caesar the privilege of permanently wearing a laurel crown. The Emperor Augustus enjoyed the same prerogative; he appreciated this, it was said, just as much as he feared

Indian capital with an acanthus decoration. While the acanthus did inspire ornamental motifs in India, it is mainly connected to the Corinthian capital, designed or merely improved by the sculptor Callimachus of Athens (5th century BC). This capital features a basket decorated with acanthus leaves.

The Acanthus: a Legend in Art

The origins of the Corinthian capital arose from an amusing legend. The Roman architect Vitruvius repeated it in the 1st century BC: 'A young Corinthian girl had died, and her nurse, who loved her very much, placed a basket on her tomb which contained various objects belonging to the deceased, and on it she laid a large flat brick to protect it from the rain.

'By chance, an acanthus seed germinated at this place, and after some time the leaves grew and surrounded the basket. The sides of the brick got in their way and gently turned back their tips, which took on a rounded shape as they grew downwards.' Their graceful curls were then noticed by Callimachus when he walked by the tomb. These beautiful curves also inspired the Ancients to crown athletes with acanthus at the Olympic Games.

thunder, and it was a conventional wisdom that no thunderbolt should ever strike the laurel.

The Tree of Eternal Life

'I love the green laurel which, ever victorious, / Neither winter nor ice can erase its greenness / Revealing its happiness for all eternity / That neither time nor death can change.' So wrote the poet Etienne Jodelle in the 16th century. The laurel's association with eternal life, because of its evergreen nature, was in fact formerly used in Christian symbolism.

P.-J. Redouté, *Pink Laurel*.

Divine Trees

The birch was a sacred tree among the Baltic Slavs, the willow was venerated by the Lithuanians, the plane tree was honoured in Sparta, where it was associated with Helen, and in Crete where it protected the love-making of Zeus and Europa... It is rare to find a tree which long ago did not have a divine attachment.

The deceased kneeling before a date palm and drinking from a pond. Tomb of Iry-Nufer, west of Thebes. 19th Dynasty.

The Tree of Buddhist Wisdom

When Siddharta became the monk Gautama, he lived in several hermitages to learn wisdom with the yogis, then he went to the sacred fig tree. Seating himself beneath the tree, he uttered the following vow: 'Here, where I sit, may my body dry up, and my skin and flesh dissolve if, before I acquire the knowledge which is so difficult to acquire in the space of many *kalpas*, I raise my body from this seat!' The earth then trembled six times. The demon Mara tried in vain to prevent him from realising his vow, but was defeated before sunset. Siddharta received perfect enlightenment and became Buddha.

The 'Patricians of the Plant World'

This was the name Linnaeus gave to the palm trees which, several decades later, Alexander von Humboldt also greatly admired. In his *Aspects of Nature* (1808) he wrote: 'Of all the plants, they are the tallest and the most noble; this is why people prized them for their beauty, and it was in the palm-growing region of Asia and neighbouring lands that the first human civilisation came into being.' This desert tree is certainly most attractive. It became the emblem of Judaea and its branches were waved to celebrate the triumphal entry of Jesus into Jerusalem, the Sunday before Easter. This is probably why it was one of Apollo's favourite trees.

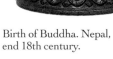

Birth of Buddha. Nepal, end 18th century.

Above:
Nicholas de Verdun, *Entry of Jesus into Jerusalem*. Retable from Verdun (detail), 1181. Stiftskirche, Klosterneuburg.

Left:
Alexandre Abel de Pujol, *Birth of Diana and Apollo*, 1822–1825. Château de Fontainebleau. Perhaps it was beneath a palm tree that Leto, whose sister was transformed into a quail by her lover, Zeus, gave birth to Apollo and Artemis on the island of Delos, which Poseidon had made rise from the sea for the occasion. Others claim instead that it was under an olive tree, another of the trees dedicated to the king of the gods.

'I Die if I Cling Not'

That is the motto of the ivy, which hooks its climbing stems onto walls and tree trunks... anywhere it can secure a hold, even in the tiniest hollow. In its illustrious past it was associated with glory: it crowned the winners of poetry competitions in Ancient Athens. It was also the emblem of Dionysus; the ivy also appeared to Cadmus to save the infant god from thunder. It is therefore not surprising that, in Rome, ivy was one of the attributes of Bacchus; a crown made from its leaves was worn by all those participating in the Bacchanalian revels.

In Lydia, the Plane Tree of the 'King of Kings'

'He [Xerxes] stopped for a whole day in this place, without anything forcing him to do so. He pitched his camp in this deserted place, around a plane tree, hung precious ornaments from it and golden bracelets. When he went away, he entrusted its safety to one of the Immortals. It was certainly a very ridiculous thing for this prince to do, a man who did not respect divine power neither at sea nor on earth, and who dared to force his way by new routes and set unknown courses, to be somehow the slave and admirer of a tree.'

Aelianus, 2nd century.

The Olive: Tree of Athene

Its twisted trunk and graceful silvery foliage link it intimately to the Mediterranean countryside. Its exceptional longevity preserves the memory of far-off times when man still worshipped plants, like the gods they were attributed to in myths.

Origins of the Olive Tree

Legend has it that Athene, goddess of the peaceful arts, disagreed with Poseidon, god of the sea, about the control of Attica. It was decided that it would go to the one who produced the most useful thing for its capital, whose name they would then take. Standing on the Acropolis, Poseidon produced a horse from the earth, according to some, or a cloth dipped in salt water, according to others. Athene made an olive tree grow in full fruit. The tree was unanimously agreed on by the gods, and the goddess became the patron of Attica. Thus Athens was 'born', and the olive became the tree of Athene for the Greeks, and that of Minerva for the Romans.

Detail of a Roman mosaic from Tunisia, decorated with the symbols of peace, a dove between two olive branches. Musée du Moyen Age-Cluny, Paris.

Above right:
Hans Memling, *Angel Holding an Olive Branch*, 15th century. Musée du Louvre, Paris.

Wisdom and Peace

The olive has remained the emblem of peace, and the wisdom that governs it, up to our own times. Throughout history it was the 'symbol of suppliants and those seeking a truce' (Emile Littré). Probably this accounts for the Ancients' custom of putting a crown of olive branches on the heads of victors, particularly during the Olympic Games.

In the Bible, the olive has a comparable meaning. It was a fresh olive leaf that the dove carried in its beak to Noah, meaning that 'the waters were abated from off the earth' (*Genesis*, 11).

It is not surprising that the oil taken from the fruit of the olive tree should have soothing, even purifying qualities. At certain Catholic and Orthodox ceremonies, the holy oil used for the unctions is a mixture of olive oil and balsam.

A Strong Symbolism

However, the message conveyed by the olive tree and its oil is often more complex. After Jacob dreamt that the God of Abraham had spoken to him, he took the stone which had been his pillow and 'set it up for a pillar, and poured oil upon the top of it', then he vowed that if God helped him and looked after him on his journey, he would make the pillar into a House of God. On the other hand, the vision of the lamp framed by two olive trees, as told in the *Book of Zechariah*, is explained in the text. The 'two olive branches which through the two golden pipes empty the golden oil out of themselves' are 'the two anointed ones, that stand by the LORD of the whole earth', that is, according to the commentary by Canon Crampon, 'the two anointed ones are the two representatives of the priesthood, Yehoshua [Joshua] and Zerubbabel'.

Below:
Lucca della Robbia, *Christ on the Mount of Olives*, 15th century. Musée du Louvre, Paris. The olive tree has a great Christian, and also Islamic, significance: it is the source of light, and symbol of the Prophet.

The Blessed Tree

'God is the light
    of the heavens and earth!
His light is comparable
    to a niche
    where a lamp stands.
The lamp is in a glass;
the glass is like
    a brilliant star.

This lamp is lit
    by a blessed tree:
The olive tree, which comes
    neither from the East
    nor from the West,
and whose oil is ready to light
    without fire touching it.

Light on light!
God guides, towards his light,
    whoever he wishes.
God proposes parables
    to men.
God knows
    all things.'

The Koran.

Emblematic Plants

Some plants make us immediately think of a quality, an idea or a country that they represent so strongly as to be inseparable from it. The role they are appointed to play may belong to one of several areas, from the spiritual to the political, from religion to folklore. The plant acts as a rallying point and takes on a quite emblematic meaning.

The Traditional Flowers of the Fields

The modest poppy and the cornflower are the popular symbols of country life and summer's richness. They are associated with the white flower of the marguerite, and were often used in France, at the end of the 19th century, for patriotic compositions displaying the tricolour.

Right:
J.-J. Grandville, 'Poppy and Cornflower' in *Les Fleurs Animées*, 1847. Bibliothèque Forney, Paris.

Previous pages:
Johann Peter Hasenclever, *80th Birthday*, 1849. Kunsthandel, Düsseldorf.

The Poppy: Red with Confusion

Where have the poppy fields gone that were so dear to Monet? Modern agricultural practices have banished the little wild poppy (*Papaver rhoeas*) from the cornfields, where once its scarlet petals twinkled over vast horizons. In French it takes its name, *coquelicot*, from the cry of the cockerel, whose red breast is a similar colour. Although the flower is not good for cutting, because it fades quickly, it was long used for beneficial purposes.

As an infusion, with added sugar, it was a remedy for colds, chest inflammations and stubborn coughs. On a more tasty note, it is still used to add scent to a boiled sweet redolent with the flavours of childhood.

The Cornflower: Simple Flower of the Virgin

The cornflower (*Centaurea cyanus*), a relative of the knapweeds and star thistles, was once a common sight in cornfields, where it grew spontaneously alongside the poppy. According to a Thessalian legend, its learned name comes from the centaur Chiron, who was very keen on botany and passed on his knowledge of medicinal plants to some famous disciples such as Aesculapius, Ulysses and Achilles.

The cornflower is the symbol of Mary. 'She is the cornflower, blue as the sky, because after her death she was planted in the celestial garden and there, after being crowned Queen of the Heavens, she was dressed by the angels in a royal blue cloak,' wrote Leo Wuyts.

Like the poppy, the cornflower was quickly seen as good for human health, particularly for the eyes. Its flowers are used to make a cornflower water, which is both astringent and refreshing. This, after being distilled 'with snow water', or so they said in the 19th century, was known as *glasses-breaking water*, for it was good for the sight.

The Cornflowers

'While the scentless star
That summer mingles with
  the blond corn-stalks,
Spangles with its lapis blue
The furrows that the crops
  turn to gold
Before its flowers are lost,
And the fields have felt
  the sickles,
Go, go, young girls,
Pick cornflowers
  in the fields!'

Victor Hugo,
Les Orientales, XXXII.

Porcelain cup and saucer decorated with cornflowers. 18th century, Paris. Musée Adrien-Dubouché, Limoges.

Flowers in Society

*In Germany at the end
of the 18th century, a
symbolic language of
flowers appeared, for use
by the society of the day.
Its delicate, playful and
somewhat precious
manner became fashionable
in the 1870s and spread
throughout Europe.*

A Hidden Meaning

This richly subtle floral language
was the preserve of those in the
know. It drew its roots from
ancient traditions which still
associated flowers with human
emotions, joy and pain. In the
Orient, a faded rose thrown by
a woman through the grille of
her window showed her sadness
at the passing of a friend (or
lover). A rose and a marguerite
(or daisy) expressed compassion.
In the West in the Middle Ages,
a lady showed a courtly knight that she was taking time to
consider his homage by wearing a crown of white daisies;
a crown of roses indicated a favourable response.

When Superstition is Involved

Today, the language of flowers can seem outdated, and it is
difficult to use because certain flowers have several meanings,
and the two protagonists need to be using the same code to
understand each other. The rules of this game still contain a
few survivors, however. It is customary not to give red roses
to a young woman, or yellow roses to a married woman, or
carnations to artists, for the flower once had a name for
attracting unfavourable reviews. Chrysanthemums also have
a taboo; once known as 'widows' flowers', they still carry a
strong whiff of the funeral, so much so that it is best not to
give them to anyone.

Above right:
Congratulations!,
1840. Coll. AKG,
Berlin.

Flowers for Special Occasions

Although they were once very strict, the rules of etiquette in the matter of flowers have lost their impact. When a baby was born, the young mother received delicately coloured, almost odourless bouquets. A baptism called for white flowers; a first communion, virginal flowers (daisy, lilac, rose, hyacinth, lily of the valley, etc.). For an engagement, the young man gave his beloved a white bouquet, while flowers with soft colours were permitted for other bouquets. A bridegroom gave his wife a bouquet that matched her outfit. White flowers were de rigueur both in church and for decorating the table for the wedding feast.

For wedding anniversaries: at silver weddings, pansies, violets and tea roses haloed with silver spikes had the place of honour; at golden weddings, yellow or orangey flowers enhanced by gold spikes; and for diamond weddings, red roses and pansies accompanied by crystal spikes.

A Specific Number

It is customary to give an odd number of roses if there are fewer than ten. Above ten, it is more complicated. 12 roses for a thank-you; 24 for flirting, and 36 for an avowal of love.

Below:
Johann Michael Voltz, *The Day of the Birth*, Nuremburg, c. 1830. At one time, the meaning of flowers could be reversed according to how they were presented. Upright for the conventional meaning, and upside down for the opposite.

The Poetic Language of Flowers and Plants

'In the world, we attribute our affections to colours (those of flowers): hope, if it is green; innocence if white; modesty if it is pink; whole nations have this integrated in their senses; a charming book which includes no dangerous errors, and keeps only the fugitive history of the heart's revolutions.' Châteaubriand.

In other words...

ABSINTH: absence.

ACACIA, WHITE FLOWER OF: desire to please, pure love.

ACHILLEA: war.

ACONITE: false security.

AGERATUM: trust.

ALMOND TREE, FLOWER OF: gentleness, absent-mindedness.

ALOE: pain, bitterness.

AMARYLLIS: artifice.

ANEMONE: abandon.

ANTHEMIS: love is over.

ARTEMISIA: conjugal fidelity, happiness.

ARUM LILY: a trap.

ASPHODEL: lost love.

ASTER: trusting love, esteem.

AZALEA: love of love.

BALSAM: anxiety, fragility.

BASIL: hatred.

BEGONIA: cordial friendship.

BINDWEED: idolising love.

BORAGE: brusqueness.

BROOM: propriety.

BUTTERCUP: ingratitude, mockery, reproach.

CACTUS: a strange nature.

CAMOMILE: submission.

CARNATION, RED: pure and ardent love.

CENTAURY: a message of love.

CHERRY TREE, FLOWER OF: good education.

CHRYSANTHEMUM: love is over.

CINERARIA: grace, heart pain.

CLEMATIS: desire, bonds.

COLUMBINE: madness.

CONVOLVULUS: coquetry.

CORNFLOWER: richness, timid love, delicacy.

CROCUS: anxiety.

CYCLAMEN: tenderness, jealousy.

CYPRESS: sadness, grief.

DAFFODIL: languorous love, desire.

DAHLIA: recognition.

DAISY: attachment.

DIGITALIS: ardour, work.

DOG ROSE: love, poetry.

EDELWEISS: noble memory of a past love.

EVERLASTING FLOWER: eternal regrets.

FORGET-ME-NOT: faithful memory.

FRENCH MARIGOLD: separation.

FUCHSIA: warm-hearted.

GARDENIA: sincerity.

GENTIAN: contempt.

GERANIUM: honesty, loving feeling.

GLADIOLUS: indifference.

GOLDEN ROD: greed.

HAWTHORN: prudence, hope.

HEATHER: solitude, solid love.

HELIOTROPE: attachment.

HELLEBORE: a lively mind.

HOLLYHOCK: uncomplicated love.

HONEYSUCKLE: friendship, love.

HORTENSIA: indifference.

HOP: injustice.

HYACINTH: kindness, light-heartedness.

IRIS: weakness, tender heart, trusting love.

JASMINE: voluptuous love.

LABURNUM: deception.

It used to be essential for a bride to carry orange flowers, and give one to each of her women friends.

LARKSPUR: lightness.

LAUREL: glory.

LAVENDER: respectful tenderness.

LILAC, WHITE: gracefulness, freshness.

LILY: purity.

LILY OF THE VALLEY: youthful ardour, flirtatiousness, return of happiness.

LIVERWORT: trust.

MAGNOLIA: strength.

MARGUERITE: kindness.

MARIGOLD: anxiety.

MIGNONETTE: modesty.

MIMOSA: safety.

MISTLETOE: invulnerability, love triumphant.

MOCK ORANGE: memory, brotherly love.

NARCISSUS: self-love, selfishness.

OLIVE TREE: peace.

ORANGE TREE, FLOWER OF: purity, generosity.

ORCHID: fervour.
PANSY: affectionate thought.
PEONY: sincerity, shame.
PERIWINKLE: melancholy, lasting friendship.
PETUNIA: obstacle.
PHLOX: flame.
POPPY: beauty.
POPPY, COLOURED: evening.
POPPY, WHITE: morning.
PRIMROSE: first love, sincere affection.
RHODODENDRON: elegance.
ROSE, CHINA: sympathy.

with love, wisdom.
ROSE, YELLOW: infidelity.
SCABIOUS: sadness
SNAPDRAGON: desires.
SNOWDROP: consolation.
SWEET PEA: delicacy.
SWEET WILLIAM: admiration.
THISTLE: austerity.
TUBEROSE: desire.
TULIP: pride.

VIOLET: modesty, secret love.
WALLFLOWER: promptness.
WATER LILY: indifference.
WISTARIA: tenderness.
ZINNIA: weakness.

GIVING FLOWERS MEANS TO SAY…
AMARYLLIS, RED: 'I respect you.'
ANEMONE: 'I trust in my love.'
ANTHEMIS: 'Goodbye!'

ROSE, ENGLISH: love.
ROSE, PINK: a pledge of love.
ROSE, RED: virtue, ardent love.
ROSE, TEA: pleasure.
ROSE, WHITE: sighing

ARUM LILY: 'Despite your problems, don't lose heart!'
BELLFLOWER: 'Why do you make me suffer?'
BOX TREE: 'I am very resistant.'
BROOM: 'You can't love twice.'
BUTTERCUP: 'I am happy to love you.'
CAMELIA, PINK: 'I am proud of your love.'
CAMELIA, RED: 'You are very beautiful.'
CAMELIA, WHITE: 'You spurn my love.'
CARNATION: 'You have a rival.'
CHRYSANTHEMUM, RED: 'I am in love.'

CYCLAMEN: 'Your beauty drives me to despair!'

DAISY: 'I want to be friends with you.'

DOG ROSE: 'I am dying of jealousy.'

FORGET-ME-NOT: 'Do not forget me'.

GENTIAN: 'Thank you.'

GLOBEFLOWER: 'You are ungrateful.'

GUELDER-ROSE: 'I am proud to love you.'

HOP: 'I can't wait to kiss you.'

HORTENSIA: 'Your whims annoy me.'

JASMINE: 'I respect you: I don't love you.'

JUNIPER: 'Passed!' 'I will try.'

LARKSPUR: 'I am very busy.'

LILAC, MAUVE: 'My heart is yours.'

LILAC, WHITE: 'Let's fall in love.'

LILY OF THE VALLEY: 'I have loved you for a long time.'

MARGUERITE: 'I see only you.'

MIGNONETTE: 'I love and hope.'

MIMOSA: 'No one knows I love you.'

NARCISSUS: 'Don't forget me!'

NASTURTIUM: 'You are indifferent!'

NETTLE: 'It's hopeless! I don't like you!'

PANSY. 'All my thoughts are of you.'

PERIWINKLE: 'I only dream of you.'

PHLOX, RED: 'I'm on fire with love for you.'

POPPY: 'Let's fall in love now!' 'I dream of you.'

ROSE, PINK: 'I love you.'

ROSE, RED: 'I am madly in love with you.'

ROSE, WHITE: 'I can't!' 'I'm fond of you.'

ROSE, YELLOW: 'You are fickle.'

SWEET PEA: 'I don't believe you.'

SWEET WILLIAM: 'I am your slave.'

THISTLE: 'Your words pain me.'

TULIP: 'You can see I love you.'

VIOLET: 'Why so modest? Be bold!'

WALLFLOWER: 'I'd like to be close to you,' 'I am faithful to you,' 'I am disappointed!'

ZINNIA: 'You don't love me any more!'

'Is your freshness a secret? Is your perfume a language?'
Alfred de Musset.

Trees and Countries

Many plants are associated with the image of a country, or even a continent. Over the centuries, trees have become national emblems, established by religion and history. More important still, they transcend all borders and have become rooted in our universal culture.

The Fig Tree of the Pharaohs

The sycamore fig tree (*Ficus sycomorus*) is a magnificent tree found in paintings of Biblical and Oriental scenes. It has strong boughs and thick foliage, and with age can reach a considerable size. It is the foremost tree in Egypt. Its fruits are not particularly tasty but are very refreshing. Mainly, though, it is the tree's light and durable wood that always made it attractive to man. In Ancient Egypt, it was used to make coffins, furniture, and even statues. Later, the Arabs used it to decorate their mosques.

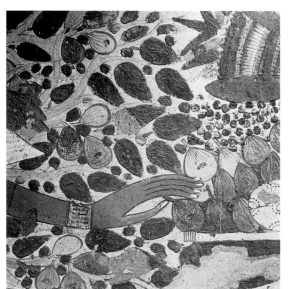

The Spectacle of Trees in Flower

The silhouette of the Japanese flowering cherry tree is often twisted and knotty, and still bare of leaves until, at the end of winter, its delicate pink flowers bloom – a sight that has inspired many Asian painters and writers. In China, where it is revered as much as the cypresses in sacred enclosures, this ornamental tree is, with

Left:
A dish of figs in an Egyptian fresco from the 14th century BC. Tomb of Sheikh Abd el-Qurnah, west of Thebes.

the pine and the bamboo, one of the 'three friends of winter'. It is a symbol of fertility, combining durability (it can reach a great age) with vitality (it is reborn just after the cold season) and purity (it flowers without leaves). The five petals of its flower correspond to the five gods of goodness. The Immortals, too, feed on its flowers. Simply to contemplate it in the moonlight is a source of joy and serenity. This practice is found in Japan, where small pavilions are built in the gardens for contemplating the moon, nature... and the cherry trees. 'Without wine, who could really enjoy the sight of the cherry trees in flower?' runs

Cherry trees in flower in one of the *Famous Sites of the Capital of the East (Toto-meisho)*, by the Japanese master Ando Hiroshige (1831–1832). Musée des Arts Asiatiques-Guimet, Paris.

a Japanese saying. The Japanese cherry is perfect for contemplation, an act that has been accompanied by wine since the 5th century, when an emperor, contemplating some wild cherry trees, watched as some petals fell into his wine cup and felt tremendous pleasure at this marriage between the drink and the evanescent beauty of the petals.

The Chinese National Tree

Rarely has a tree been so useful. In China the bamboo, symbol of resistance and robustness, is part of every person's life until their last dwelling place, when it joins the cypresses, junipers and pines around the tomb. Its uses are in fact enormous: hats, shoe

Opposite bottom: Lou Tche, fan decorated with cherry flowers, China, 1570. Musée des Arts Asiatiques-Guimet, Paris.

Above: Tomb of Neferhetep, Thebes, 18th Dynasty. The papyrus, a plant of Ancient Egypt, inspired painters and architects.

Right: Tomioka Tessai, *Red Bamboos and Black Mountains*, Japan, 19th century. Musée des Arts Asiatiques-Guimet, Paris.

soles, pipes, baskets, sieves, pencil-holders, measuring instruments, brooms, tubes, stakes and trellises in the garden, fishing rods, boat sails, aqueducts, agricultural tools, building material, furniture...
Its shavings were once used to make pillows, and its leaves a sort of cape for keeping off the rain. Chopsticks, indispensable at mealtimes and used instead of knives and forks, are made of bamboo. In short, Chinese life is inconceivable without bamboo.

In the Heart of Winter, the *Nandina domestica*

'The Chinese call it "tein-chok", or sacred bamboo, and collect many branches from the countryside at that time, so that the streets are full of them. Each of these branches is crowned with a large bouquet of red berries, very like those of our holly. The contrast with the dark, shiny leaves is very decorative. It is mainly used for decorating altars, not only in temples but also in homes and boats. Here, in fact, every house and every boat has an altar. That is why it is called the sacred bamboo.'

Robert Fortune,
A Journey to the Tea Countries of China,
1852.

The Cedar: Strength and Majesty

'All the Arab sects feel a traditional reverence for these trees; they admire them not only for the physical strength which makes them live for ever, but also see in them a soul which imparts signs of wisdom and prediction [...].'
Lamartine

Below:
Building the Temple of Solomon, anonymous 16th-century engraving. Bibl. Nat., Paris.

Opposite above:
Louis-François Cassas, *The Forest of Cedars in the Second Region of Lebanon,* c. 1800. Bibl. Mazarine, Paris.

A Myth in Egypt

Legend has it that the Egyptian god Osiris was shut in a chest by his brother Set, who was jealous of his power, and the chest was thrown into the river. Isis, his wife, found this coffin at Byblos, in Phoenicia, in the trunk of a tree that a king had used to support the roof of his palace. Some maintain that it was a tamarisk, others an umbrella pine, and yet others a cedar – and probably this last version of the myth is the most likely.

A Contemporary of the Age of the Bible

The Scriptures celebrate the cedar of Lebanon in several places. King Solomon used it to build the Temple of Jerusalem, which he built to the one God; he clad the interior walls with cedar and had it carved 'with gourds and open flowers: all was in cedar; there was no stone seen' (*First Book of Kings*). The altar of the sanctuary was in cedar covered with gold. He also used it for the roof, the columns and the Judgment Portico of his 'house from the Forest of Lebanon'. In *The Book of Psalms*, the tree is made a symbol: 'The righteous shall flourish like the palm tree: he shall grow like a cedar in Lebanon' (92, 12). 'The voice of the LORD breaketh the cedars; yea, the LORD breaketh the cedars of Lebanon' (29, 5).

Immortal in Lebanon

The image of the cedars standing proudly on top of the mountains of Lebanon is rich in poetry. But these trees have gradually diminished in number. The rare survivors are the witnesses of ages past.

An Ancient Reverence

The Ancients thought the cedar was a symbol of immortality. The Egyptians used its durable and scented wood to make statues of gods and sarcophagi. They also attributed divinatory powers to it – its Egyptian name, *ash*, means 'to tremble'. The Greeks burnt its wood at non-bloody sacrifices. The Asians revered it on a secular level. In China, it was planted in sacred enclosures. In Japan, it was also highly prized by Buddhist monks and traditionally stood inside sanctuaries.

In his day, Alphonse de Lamartine strongly expressed the feeling he had after seeing the cedars of Lebanon. His words seem very modern today: 'Every year, in the month of June, the peoples of Beschieraï, Eden, Kanobin and all the villages in the nearby valleys climb up to the cedars and hold a mass beneath them. So many prayers have echoed through these branches! What more beautiful temple, what altar could be closer to heaven! What more majestic and saintly dais than the upper plateau of Lebanon, the trunks of the cedars and the domes of these sacred branches which have given shade to, and still give shade to, so many human generations uttering the name of God differently, but seeing him everywhere in his works, and adoring him in his natural manifestations!'

Sarcophagus of the lady Madja, excavated at Deir el-Medinah, 18th Dynasty. Musée du Louvre, Paris.

The Lily: Purity and Nobility

Jupiter gave Heracles permission to suck the sleeping Hera's breast to make himself immortal. The child sucked so hard that the divine milk spurted out and formed the Milky Way. The lily grew from a drop which fell back to earth. Aphrodite, jealous of its whiteness, gave the flower an enormous pistil, which some have likened to a donkey's phallus.

Right: Eustache Le Sueur, *La Salutation Angélique*, c. 1650. Musée du Louvre, Paris.

The Choice of Being Loved

[THE WIFE]
'I am the rose of Sharon,
and the lily of the valleys.'

[THE HUSBAND]
'As the lily among
thorns,
so is my love among
the daughters.'
The Song of Solomon

Virginal Innocence

Emphasising that its smooth scent is strongest in the evening, Pierre Leuthaghi saw it as a 'flower of dusk which, more than any other, brings brightness to the night, and its most penetrating scent.' He added: 'Thus it belongs naturally to the place where spirits and simple souls are found. On the altar of the divinities (with us, the Virgin Mary) and on the tombs of young girls, it demonstrates the eternal benefits of purity.' Since the Romans, in fact, the colour white has been associated with purity and virginity. This symbolism, featuring the white lily, often appears in religiously inspired paintings, particularly Flemish and Italian works.

In works representing the Annunciation, the angel Gabriel offers a lily to the Virgin. More often, a vase contains one or several lilies. Sometimes, three lily branches embody Mary's triple virginity, before, during and after the birth of Jesus. Occasionally, the flower is associated with the iris, as in the *Virgin and Four Saints* (c. 1450) by Rogier Van der Weyden. It is mixed with roses in *The Virgin Infant* (17th century) by Francisco de Zurburán.

Rogier Van der Weyden, *Virgin and Four Saints*, c. 1450. Städelsches Kunstinstitut, Frankfurt.

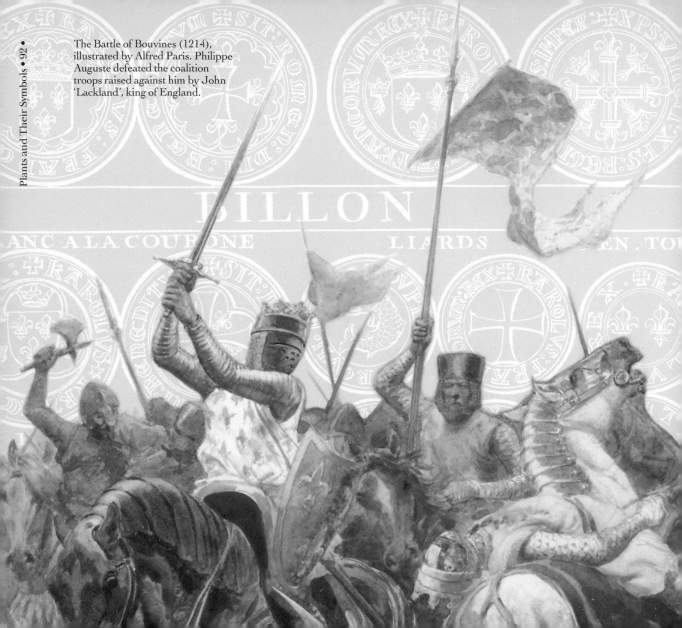

The Battle of Bouvines (1214), illustrated by Alfred Paris. Philippe Auguste defeated the coalition troops raised against him by John 'Lackland', king of England.

Passignano, posthumous portrait of *Cosmo I de Médicis, Duke of Florence and Grand-Duke of Tuscany*, 1597. Opificio delle Pietre Dure, Florence.

A Noble Flower

In heraldry, the lily is a symbol of glory and fertility. In addition, according to G.A. Böckler (Nuremberg, 1688), it is royal because its shape is like that of a sceptre, and also because its 'delectable scent' keeps serpents at bay. It appeared in large numbers on the French crown in the middle of the 12th century, and soon became the symbol of royalty. In the *Annals* of the city of Nangis, it states: 'The kings of France took to wearing on their arms the lilies as though they ruled the world: Faith, Wisdom and Chivalry were, by the provision and grace of God, more abundant in our kingdom than in any other.' Louis VII reduced the number of flowers to three. From the second half of the 14th century, the arms were 'azure with three golden lilies'. It should also be mentioned that the heraldic flower of the House of France only bears the name lily. Although Voltaire would have liked it to show 'the tip of a halberd', it shows the marsh lily with large yellow flowers and sword-shaped leaves. For the marriage of Henry II and Catherine de Médicis, the lily was also adopted by the arms of the Médicis. It later featured in the coat of arms of Tuscany. The escutcheon of Florence bore the red lily which is also thought of as the symbol of the Passion.

Grandeur and Decadence

The Madonna lily (*Lilium candidum* L.) originally came from the Orient, and for a long time was cultivated for its ornamental beauty and penetrating scent. A painted stucco relief, found in Knossos and featuring a priest-king or a royal knight, proves the nobility of this flower in pre-Hellenic times. Among the Ancients and in the Middle Ages, it took pride of place in gardens, where it was often planted next to roses. The fashion for it declined rapidly in the 16th century, when the lily of Chalcedon (*Lilium chalcedonicum*), also called the Scarlet Turk's Cap, was imported from Turkey and its red flowers were all the rage.

Strong Emblems for Harsh Regions

Saint Patrick used the clover to illustrate the mystery of the Holy Trinity while he was evangelising in Ireland. The thistle grows everywhere in Scotland and is part of the country's image. In addition to their emblematic value, these two plants have provoked a variety of interpretations, often tinged with mysticism.

Midnight on New Year's Eve.
Postcard, 1904.

The Clover: Vitality and Goodness

Who has not looked in the fields for a four-leafed clover? The plant only has three leaflets, as its learned name *Trifolium* indicates. But, thanks to a peculiarity of nature, it can sometimes have four. It is very rare, and for that reason can only be a sign of good luck. Among the Celts, the Druids believed that the four-leafed clover gave its owner the gift of seeing demons, and this allowed him to save himself from them with incantations.

A Mystical Connotation

The clover, in the form of the shamrock, is the emblem of Ireland, and over the years has acquired various symbolic meanings. It stands for an intense lifestyle, by virtue of its vigorous nature. Also for separation and rebirth – it was used to decorate tombs. In Christian terms, it represents the divine Trinity – in religious architecture its leaf has inspired trefoil forms and motifs. In the Middle Ages, the minstrels singing of courtly love claimed that the presence of the 'green clover' encouraged love affairs.

The Thistle: Protection and Grief

The thistle has always been a symbol of resistance, and among the Ancients it was used for keeping demons at bay.

They also credited it with various therapeutic benefits.
The variety *Centum capita* was said to arouse passion in a
loved-one. In some regions, it was once used as a barometer,
and people hung it on their front doors. If it opened, fine
weather was on the way.

The Sign of the Virgin

In Western Christianity, the
Blessed Thistle is a sign of
suffering; its spines recall the
Passion of Christ. The Milk
Thistle, once known as the
Lady's Thistle or the Notre-
Dame Thistle, has very large
leaves veined with white,
which represent the drops of
mother's milk which fell as the
Virgin was hiding Jesus from
Herod's soldiers.

Immortality
and Memory

The trees that lend their greenery to the last resting places of humans, and the flowers that traditionally decorate tombs, were not chosen by chance. They often relate to customs begun by the Ancients, who appointed this or that plant to symbolise sadness, death or grief, and the idea of returning to the light in the beyond.

The Columbine: the Virgin's Flower

*'The anemone and the
columbine
Grew in the garden
Where melancholy sleeps
Between love and contempt.'*
                Guillaume Apollinaire

Previous pages: Edgar Degas, *Woman
with Chrysanthemums* (detail), 1865.
Coll. H.O. Havemeyer, Metropolitan
Museum of Art, New York.

Below: Albrecht Dürer, *Columbine*,
16th century. Graphische Sammlung
Albertina, Vienna.

Eagle or Dove?

According to Albertus Magnus (13th century), the plant's
Latin name *aquilegia* was derived from *aquila* (eagle), a reminder
that some botanists had detected the bird of prey's silhouette in
the spurs of its five petals. This was a somewhat fantastic
interpretation because the plant's original Latin name was in
fact *aquilegus*, 'which collects water', because of its bell-shaped
flowers. Ecclesiastical authors prefer the silhouette of a dove to
that of an eagle, the form in which the Holy Spirit is traditionally
represented. For this reason, in the Middle Ages, the columbine
was also called *columbina*. This was probably the 'dove flower'
that Albrecht Dürer painted in watercolour on parchment in
1520.

A Subtle Flower

In religious imagery, the columbine (*Aquilegia vulgaris*) stands,
like the violet, for the humility of virgins and martyrs. The
flower's emblematic value interested painters in the Middle
Ages and the Renaissance. Many paintings with a religious
theme employed it, either for *The Adoration of the Shepherds* or
the *Virgin and Child*. In the latter, the flower is the attribute of
Mary, signalling both her purity and the Holy Ghost, which
appeared during the Annunciation.

Beneficial Properties

'This plant,' the *Nouvelle Maison Rustique* (1804) tells us,
'stimulated the appetite, and was diuretic, sudorific, detersive
and a remedy for scurvy. A small amount of its powdered
root, taken in wine, soothed colic in the kidneys, and a small
amount of its powdered seed, mixed with a little saffron and taken

Circle of Master François,
The Annunciation, book of hours,
second half of 15th century.
Musée des Beaux-Arts, Lille.

The Bumblebee

'Beside a dusty road I found a plant with a flower that was both brilliant and dark, ideal for sharing in the most noble and pure forms of grief. It was a columbine. Our fathers called it the glove of Notre-Dame. A Notre-Dame [Our Lady] that could make herself very small, to appear to children, and could only slip her tiny fingers into the narrow capsules of this flower. 'Now a fat bumblebee is burrowing brutally into the flower; it cannot reach the nectar with its mouth despite its greedy efforts. It gives up at last and emerges covered in pollen. [...] It comes back to the columbine, and this time breaks the corolla and sucks the nectar through the opening it has made; I would not have thought a bumblebee would have had so much sense.'
Anatole France,
Le Crime de Sylvestre Bonnard.

in a glass of wine, was very good for jaundice. A tincture made from its flowers and spirits of wine was excellent for cleaning the mouth and strengthening the gums.' In addition to its therapeutic qualities, columbine was regarded as a cure for meanness.

The Cypress: Tree of Sorrow

One day, Cyparissus killed his most faithful companion, a sacred stag, by mistake. In his grief, he wanted to kill himself. Apollo loved the young man, and tried to console him. Nothing worked. He transformed himself into a tree, and Apollo gave it the symbol of inconsolable sorrow. Thus the cypress came into being.

Earthenware jug from Iznik, Turkey. 14th–15th centuries. Musée d'Ecouen.

Above right:
Giovanni Mattei, *Cyparissus Turned into a Cypress*, 1651. Bibliothèque des Arts Décoratifs, Paris.

Grief and Long Life

In Antiquity, the cypress was associated with hell and the cult of the dead, and was planted close to tombs. This custom continues today, conferring also the Christian message of hope in the everlasting. In the Far East, where it is found in sacred enclosures, the tree has always been linked to the notion of immortality, because of its evergreen foliage. In Japan, Shinto rites use a variety of cypress, the *kinoki*, a symbol of incorruptibility and purity.

Left: Alessio Baldovinetti, *Madonna with Eight Saints*, c. 1454. Uffizi Gallery, Florence.

Below: Alexander consulting the Tree of the Sun and the Moon in Jansen Enikel, *Chroniques du Monde*. Bibliothèque Forney, Paris.

Loves of Cassandra

'It could happen
   that a poet in love,
Horrified by
   my unhappy fate,
Might write this epigram
   on a cypress:
"Here beneath lies
   a lover from the Vendôme,
Killed by grief
   in this wood.
For loving the eyes
   of his lady too much."'
       Pierre de Ronsard.

Trees of the Sun and Moon

Legend has it that Alexander the Great consulted the Tree of the Sun and the Tree of the Moon which, it seems, were located in Persia. These marvellous trees, which looked like cypresses and were endowed with speech, could reply in Greek and Indian and predicted his imminent death.

In Western literature of the Middle Ages the 'romance' of Alexander was one of the favourite themes and repeated this

The Fir, Tree of Burials

Today the wood of fir trees is used to make coffins. The Ancients preferred cypress wood for this purpose, which the Athenians thought lasted forever, reported Thucydides. Pliny, however, mentions the relationship of the fir tree to death. Probably this was because it was the custom to hang branches of cypress or fir tree on the front door of the deceased.

Above:
The tomb of François Andrieux (1759–1833) in Père-Lachaise cemetery, Paris.

wonder, which in fact was inspired by an old Hindustani custom in which the natives planted two trees at the top of sacred hills where they celebrated marriages of the gods. Probably, they were palm trees which in that part of Asia were, like the cypress, dedicated to the Sun and the Moon.

The 'Cypress of the Fatal Night'

On the road to Veracruz, in Mexico, the cypress of Hernán Cortés was very old; it was still alive in 1875. It was no less than 36 metres (118 feet) in circumference. In 1520, under the command of Pedro de Alvarado, in the absence of the Conquistador, the massacre of hundreds of defenceless Indians, who had come to celebrate their god, sparked a violent revolt among the Aztecs against the Spanish. Moctezuma being dead, the latter had to flee in great confusion. Tradition has it that Cortés made his first stop in the shade of this cypress, and there he was told of the disaster suffered by his troops. On this spot he recovered the serenity and courage to organise a disciplined retreat.

The Funeral Cypress

During his journey through China described in *A Journey to the Tea Countries of China*, in the middle of the 19th century, Robert Fortune was delighted by a tree of majestic bearing which at first seemed to him to be 'a type of weeping willow', belonging to the pine family according to its foliage. The botanist brought its seeds to England, where the plant was called the *Funeral Cypress*. 'For a line time we had been sorry that the Italian cypress could not be adapted to our climate and be used in our cemeteries. Now we have a more slender tree which is much better suited to this purpose,' stated Professor Lindley.

Arnold Böcklin, *Isle of the Dead*,
1886. Museum der Bildenden
Künste, Leipzig.

The Chrysanthemum: a Scent from the Far East

'Like fires torn by a great colourist from the instability of the atmosphere and the sun, [...] these chrysanthemums invited me, despite all my sadness, avidly at that teatime hour to taste these too-short November pleasures as they blazed beside me with an intimate and mysterious splendour.'

Marcel Proust

Japanese print from the end of the 19th century. Bibl. des Arts Décoratifs, Paris.

Permanence and Beauty

In the West, the chrysanthemum is the flower of All Saints, the memory and commemoration of the dead. It thus has a powerful funerary image which tends to make us forget that in Asia its ornamental role is accompanied by a less austere symbolism. The Chinese and Japanese associate it with the idea of longevity, which its leaves, formerly used for medicinal purposes, help to bring about. While it is endowed with durability, it also represents perfect beauty and is a source of joy.

In China, the Symbol of Autumn

The chrysanthemum comes from China, where it was cultivated from the 5th century BC, and had yellow flowers, as is borne out by its Greek name, which literally means 'golden flower'. It was only from the Tang Dynasty, in the 7th century AD, that it acquired other colours and took on other forms. At the beginning of the 18th century, there were some three hundred known varieties. Many artists have painted it, and many poets have written about it. One of them, T'ao Yuan Ming, preferred growing it to receiving worldly honours. As a result, the chrysanthemum symbolises for the Chinese the renunciation of the world of profit in favour of a simpler and deeper life.

The Emblem of Imperial Japan

The chrysanthemum was introduced into Japan at the beginning of the 5th century AD, and very soon was grown with as much passion as it was in China. Thus the winter garden of Mrs Muraski

in the *Story of Genji* (11th century) contained a 'large border of chrysanthemums', ready to be admired when frost covered the garden. Because of the radiating pattern of its petals, the Japanese saw in this flower (*kiku*) a solar symbol, and even called it the 'Materialisation of the Sun'. It is hardly surprising that the mikado, a descendant of the Sun goddess Amaterasu, should take it for his emblem. This has 11 petals and features a kind of 'compass card, at the centre of which the emperor rules, embodying the direction of the space around him' (Pierre Grison).

In 1876, the Emperor Meiji Tenno created the Order of the Chrysanthemum, whose decoration was a red ribbon with violet borders.

Torii Kiyonaga (1752–1815), *Dance of the Chrysanthemums*, Japan. Musée des Arts Asiatiques-Guimet, Paris.

'The Favourite Winter Flower of the Chinese Gardener'

In this way in the middle of the 19th century, Robert Fortune described the chrysanthemum, which the Chinese cultivated with such expertise that they produced all kinds of curious shapes. The botanist claimed moreover to have seen them in the shape of animals, horses and does, and even seven-storey pagodas. Beyond this quest for novelty, the flowers were piled up in compact mounds that people drew from to decorate temples and interiors.

The Pine: Permanence and Vital Power

*'I plant in your favour
this tree of Cybele,
This pine, where your honours
can be read every day.
I engraved on the trunk
our names and our loves,
Which will vie with each other
to grow from the new bark.'
Pierre de Ronsard, poem
addressed to Hélène de
Surgères.*

Performance
of *Atys* (1676),
an opera by
Jean-Baptiste Lully.

The Tree of Cybele

In the time of the Ancients, the pine tree was dedicated to the Mother of the Gods, Cybele, daughter of Heaven and Earth. She fell in love with a shepherd, Attis, on Mount Ida, and made him guardian of her temple, provided he took a vow of chastity. The young man broke his vow by marrying the daughter of the river god Sangarius. Cybele had her rival put to death. Attis, mad with grief, emasculated himself, and the goddess turned him into a pine – probably an umbrella pine (*Pinus pinea* L.).

Opposite above:
Mosaic from Carthage showing two lions beside a pine, 550. Musée du Bardo, Tunis.

Left:
Jean-Antoine Watteau, *The Betrothal*, 18th century. Musée des Beaux-Arts, Valenciennes.

Illumination in Robert de Boron, *The Story of Merlin*. Bibl. Nat., Paris.

The Sacred Tree of Merlin

Merlin the Enchanter climbed to the top of the pine tree which stood above the fountain of Barenton, in the forest of Broceliand, and there he acquired supreme knowledge. It was a kind of cosmic tree bound to the domain of the dead through the fountain. 'From then on he lived there, for the "house of glass" [which he sought] was none other than the top of the green tree, where Merlin finally obtained all his powers...' wrote Jacques Brosse.

At first the cult of Cybele was limited to Phrygia, then was practised in Crete and introduced to Rome in the 3rd century BC. It was known for its highly licentious rites. Every year, in March at the spring equinox, ritual feasts were held at which the sacred pine, symbol of the mutilation of Attis, was brought into the Palatine temple. Blood was spread over the trunk, which was covered in bandages and decorated with violets, to resuscitate the tree-god and, as a result, bring the plants back to life.

The Black Pine of Pitys

The nymph Pitys escaped from Pan, who was trying to violate her, by transforming herself into a maritime pine or a black pine (*Pinus pinaster*). Another version of the legend claims that she gave her favours to Pan rather than Boreas, and that the latter was enraged and blew with such force that the young nymph fell over a cliff. Earth, taking pity, then changed her into a pine tree. According to P. Commelin, 'This is why this tree, which retained the nymph's feelings, crowns Pan with its foliage, while the winds of Boreas make it tremble.'

The Tree of Life

In the Far East, the long life of its needles through the seasons has made the tree come to symbolise longevity and stability. Thus it can be found everywhere in Chinese gardens. It is often allied to the bamboo and the cherry tree, which convey the same idea, forming a triad guaranteeing long life and happiness. Like the cypress, the pine (*matsu*) is used in Japan by the Shinto religion (based on the veneration of the powers of nature) to make temples and ritual instruments. It is associated both with the idea of immortality and of a return to the light.

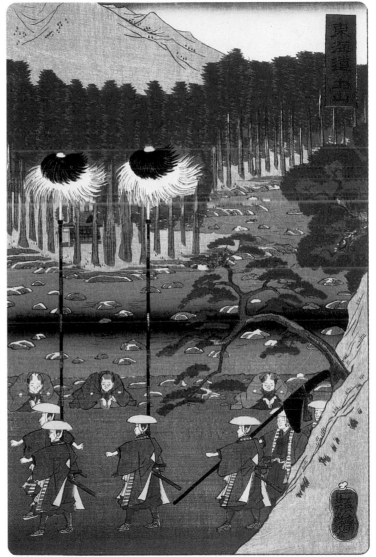

Above:
An immortal rising in the sky. China. Bibl. Nat., Paris.

Right:
Utagawa Yoshitsuya, *Station Tsuchiyama*, procession along a river. Japan, 1863. Tokaido.

The Mysterious Mandrake

Man may originally have been a gigantic mandrake which, animated by the Sun, freed itself from the earth in which its roots were buried. This idea has obsessed many people since Antiquity. It cannot be denied that this plant's strange root does lend itself to unusual interpretations.

'Little Man in the Ground'

The mandrake's root looks like the lower part of the human body. It has 'the shape of a man', said the Greek Theophrastes, or a 'half man', according to the Latin writer Columella. This likeness quickly earned it both fear and reverence. The Ancients made it an attribute of the clever magician Circe, and credited it with hundreds of therapeutic powers: as a soporific, anaesthetic, aphrodisiac, a remedy for sterility...

Alchemy and Occultism

The plant aroused even greater interest in the Middle Ages. Occult practitioners sought it out, using it particularly to make up philtres and ointments. Even Christians viewed it with some respect. In the 12th century, the Benedictine abbess Saint Hildegard wrote: 'The mandrake, with its human shape, is made from the earth where the

first man was moulded, hence it is more exposed than any other plant to the devil's temptations. Sufferers must take a mandrake root, wash it carefully, put it in their bed and recite the following prayer: O Lord, who created man from clay without pain, see that I place next to myself the same earth which has not yet sinned, that my wicked flesh may obtain the same peace that it had in the beginning.'

Sought After and Feared

The mandrake was a symbol of fertility and richness, and was once called the 'hand of glory'. It was reputed to bring happiness and good luck to its owner. It therefore became the object of a mysterious and

Above:
Digging up the mandrake according
to Boaistuau in *Histoires Prodigieuses*,
16th century.

fierce trade, often subject
to trickery. However, this
positive aspect of the plant
only came to light if one acted
cautiously. It was difficult to
obtain one. When it was
pulled up, it uttered a horrible
shriek of agony that was
deadly dangerous. So dogs
were made to dig it up,
which was the only way to
avoid the danger. Medieval
tradition also claims that the
mandrake was born from the
sperm of hanged men, and
should be picked beneath the

gallows. As Jacques Brosse
explained, 'The power of
the plant, combining death
and sexuality, rested on the
fact that this wasted sperm
would be recovered, to the
advantage of the lucky
owner of the root.'

School of Verona or Lombardy,
'Fructus Mandragore'. Illustration
in *Tacuinum Sanitatis in Medicina*
(14th century). National Library,
Vienna. Those who picked the
mandrake were careful not to
stand downwind from it.
They marked three circles round
it with a sword, then they turned
to face the setting sun and
removed the earth.'
(Pliny the Elder)

The Flowers of Memory

Their symbolism is rooted in the Western language of flowers, but is strong and lively. They induce memory and remembrance. In addition, like other flowers with five petals, they relate to man and his five senses.

J.-J. Grandville, 'The Forget-me-not' in *Les Fleurs Animées*, 1847. Bibliothèque Forney, Paris. In some Western symbols, particularly from eastern Europe, blue is the colour of fidelity. It is not surprising that the forget-me-not is linked with memory.

The Pansy: Elegant and Mysterious

The pansy of fields and gardens (*Viola tricolor* L.) is a first cousin of the violet, as its learned name indicates, and belongs to the same genus. It was Lady Mary Bennet, daughter of the Earl of Tankerville, who improved its method of cultivation, produced some interesting varieties, and in the 1810s created a remarkable collection of pansies. The 'English pansy', as it was called, had no equal for a long time, and Belgium and Germany followed England in cultivating it. Then, in 1835, a French horticulturist, M. Boursault, exhibited a collection of pansies which dethroned the English ones forever; from then on, people talked only of the 'large-flowered pansies'. The pansy symbolises meditation, richness and beauty. More important still, it is the messenger of affectionate thoughts.

The Forget-Me-Not: 'Flower of Love'

It is unusual for flowers to have such a poetic name as the forget-me-not. Although its original Greek name (*Myosotis*) means 'mouse's ear', because of the shape of the leaves, it has since acquired such charming popular names as 'love-me' and 'the-more-I-see-you-the-more-I-love-you'. The name forget-me-not was adopted by the English and the Germans (*Vergissmeinnicht*).

Several legends are connected to this plant. According to one, a forget-me-not flower was once able to show someone, who had the power to enter a château, where a vast treasure was hidden. So a man found this treasure, and filled his pockets with it, but

Right:
Spanish School,
Lady with Pansies,
15th century. Musée
du Louvre, Paris.

Opposite bottom:
The forget-me-not was
once called the 'Flower
of God' and was an
attribute of Jesus and
the Virgin. Some
medieval paintings
feature this symbol.

in his ecstasy he
left the flower
behind. The flower
then reminded him
of his ingratitude
with the words: 'Do not forget me,' which reached his ears,
and the enchanted path which had led him to this fortune
was closed to him forever.

In Germanic areas, they tell of a young man who was
carried away in a river by the current. But he managed
to grab a little blue flower from the bank and throw it at
his fiancée, crying: 'Forget me not!' before he disappeared
in the rushing waters. In England, the symbol stems from
the Duke of Lancaster who, during his exile, sent the
Duchess of Brittany a myosotis flower, which he called
'Forget me not' so that the gentle lady would remember him.

Growing Wild in the Garden

'The overflowing basins looked more like vast window boxes with crumbling, broken marble sides. In one of the biggest, a gust of wind had sown a marvellous collection of pansies. Their velvet flowers seemed almost human, with their violet headbands, yellow eyes, paler mouths and delicate flesh-coloured chins.
– When I was young, they made me afraid, murmured Albine. Look at them. Don't they look like thousands of little faces looking up at you from the ground? ... And they turn their faces all together. They are like buried dolls with just their heads poking out.'

Emile Zola,
*La Faute de
l'Abbé Mouret.*

The Plants of Mourning

The custom of leaving plants for the deceased goes back a long way. The Ancients used palms or flowers. The Christians took up this pagan tradition. In the 19th century they made elaborate compositions: round and oval wreaths, sheaves, crosses and cushions.

'A fresh scent rose
from the clumps
of asphodels...'
Victor Hugo,
Booz Endormi.

The Antique Ritual

When a family member's illness had brought them to death's door, laurel branches were hung over the front door, this being the shrub dedicated to Apollo, to place the family under the protection of the god of medicine. Once the deceased had been dressed for burial, a crown was placed on his head made up of plants (olive, laurel, white poplar, lily and ash) that reflected his social standing. In Athens, the ceremony was held at night, with flaming torches lighting the procession as they went along to the sound of flutes made of boxwood. If the body was cremated, conifer wood was used to burn the body. The ashes were collected in urns, or were mixed with perfumes of myrtle and rose, incense and violet.

Consecrated Plants

'The amaranthus stimulates a contempt for earthly things,' wrote the Jesuit father Allard Le Roy in 1641. This spiritual quality allocated to the plant, whose autumn flowers are a superb velvety purple and do not fade, dates from Ancient times when it symbolised immortality. The Greeks and Romans decorated their tombs with it, as though they were offering violets, mallows and cypress to the spirits.

The Asphodel: Flower of the Blessed Deceased

'And do not think that the beatitude of heroes and demigods in the Elysian Fields comes from their asphodels, or ambrosia or nectar, like these old women say.' This was how Rabelais

The Funeral Message

There are certain rules for sending flowers when someone has died, which reflect the symbolism of the plants concerned. If the deceased is a child, an adolescent or a young woman, the flowers must be white. They can be lilies, lilac, roses, dahlias or chrysanthemums. In other cases, the colours are not important. However, the favoured flowers are those of remembrance, like chrysanthemums, pansies, violets, lilac and roses. Foliage is also chosen for its association with remembrance, and is usually ivy, a cypress branch, thuja or pine, palm, a branch of oak or dog rose, and all the leaves that in the autumn turn a golden colour. At one time the everlasting flower, which as its name suggests, could be kept indefinitely, was used for funeral bouquets and wreaths.

Left:
Edouard Manet, *Berthe Morisot with a Bouquet of Violets*. Musée d'Orsay, Paris.

Pierre Gourdault, *Burial in Deux-Sèvres*, end of 19th century. Musée d'Orsay, Paris.

Opposite:
J.-A. Watteau, *The Elysian Fields*, 1716–1717. Gracefulness and lightness mingle with the mythic story. Wallace Collection, London.

The Tree of Tears and Sleep

On the banks of the River Chata-Uche was a wild fig tree, which was sacred to a popular cult. Virgins used to wash their dresses with bark at this place, and lay them out on branches of the old tree to blow in the desert wind. Here an enormous tomb had been dug out. The people leave the death room singing the hymn to the dead; each family carries some sacred remnant. They arrive at the tomb; they put down the relics, stretching them out in layers, separated by bear and beaver skins; they go up to the top of the tomb, and there plant *The Tree of Tears and Sleep*'

François-René de Chateaubriand, *Atala*.

Below:
China plate, 18th century, decorated with a funeral urn on the sides of which can be seen portraits of Louis XVI and Marie-Antoinette. Musée des Arts Asiatiques-Guimet, Paris.

alluded to the link between the asphodel and the resting place of the dead in Greek and Roman mythology, in *Gargantua* (XIII). Eternal spring reigned in this place of virtuous souls. Nature's fragrance hung in the air. Rose trees and myrtles formed harmonious masses. The fresh lawn was strewn with clumps of asphodels. This plant with its bright foliage and lovely bunches of starry flowers was sacred, viewed as the emblem of eternal resurrection. This it seems was the yellow asphodel (*Asphodelus luteus*), popularly known as 'Jacob's wand'. The Ancients planted it close to tombs 'as the most pleasant food for the dead' (Bouillet, *Dictionary*); they actually thought that the dead took delight in eating its roots. It is true that asphodel bulbs are fleshy, starchy and contain sugar, particularly those of the branchy asphodel (*Asphodelus ramosus*), which Pliny called the 'little sceptre' and later in the Middle Ages was known as the 'royal stick' (*Hastula regia*).

The Immortality of Hard Woods

Yew and box are, to some extent, the symbols of gardens in the French style. The former is shaped into pyramids, spheres and cones, and many other forms... The latter is also shaped by man, outlining the arabeques of decorative borders. Both, however, in addition to this noble ornamental role, convey the notion of exceptional permanence.

Above:
On Palm Sunday in Paris, at the beginning of the 20th century, in *Le Petit Journal* of Sunday, 9 April 1911. Bibl. Forney, Paris. Its slow growth gives the box an eternal character which, since Ancient times, has made its presence favourable.

The Box Tree: a Christian Shrub

In Antiquity, the box tree was dedicated both to the divinities of the underworld and Cybele, the mother-goddess, and symbolised immortality and perseverance, because of the hardness of its wood and the long life of its foliage. Christians adopted it. On Palm Sunday – also quaintly known as 'Easter in Blossom' in some countries – its branches are traditionally blessed by the priest. They are a symbol of hope and stability, and will watch over their family until the following year. Formerly, in the countryside where superstition was rife, the blessed branches protected the house against evil and storm damage. In medieval gardens, its beneficial qualities, associated with medicinal properties, probably also persuaded people to plant box to make low borders surrounding their flower beds.

The Yew: a Warlike Conifer

The yew was a symbol of immortality in Ancient times, and so became one of the plants favoured by the cult of the dead. Anatole Le Braz, who in the 1920s studied the role of death among the Bretons of the Côte d'Armor, explained that these people used to believe that there should only be one yew tree in each cemetery, for its roots grew into the mouths of all the deceased buried there. The yew is one of the great funerary trees, and the Celts also linked it to their martial pursuits. Its very hard, robust wood was used to make shields and lances. The highly toxic substance (*taxine*) contained in its red fruits was smeared on the tips of their lances to help them beat their enemies.

Above:
Gauls carrying yew shields. Terracotta, 2nd century BC. Civic Museum, Bologna.

Right:
Albrecht Dürer, *The Crucifixion*, 1495. From the *Seven Sorrows of Mary* series. Gemäldegalerie, Dresden.

The Legend of the Box Tree

'At the time when Christ died [...] the Box tree of the Upper Caucasus felt an immense sigh, like a lugubrious breeze, pass through its branches that was exhaled from the chest of the dying God, and which went from Golgotha to heaven. Horror dried the sap in its trunk; its leaves grew darker; its knotty branches rubbed against one another. Then it too murmured: "Christ is dead, and, as a sign of anguish, I will live in the uncultivated stony hills. In necropolises, my branches will line the funeral pathways. But also, as the symbol of the immortal hopes which hover over tombs, my evergreen branches, borne by Christians, will echo the triumphal entry of the Man-God into the sunny streets of Solyma."'

O. Havard,
Les Fêtes de Nos Pères,
19th century.

From Trees to Perfumes

'The introduction of incense and perfumes in our churches, so ancient and widespread among all nations and religions, is to help us rejoice; to awake and purify our senses and prepare us for contemplation.'

Montaigne, Essays.

Charles Lameire, *Christ Enthroned Between Two Angels.* Chapelle des Dames Auxiliatrices, Paris.

A Symbolic Vision

'And another angel came and stood at the altar, having a golden censer; and there was given unto him much incense, that he should offer it with the prayers of all saints upon the golden altar which was before the throne. And the smoke of the incense, which came with the prayers of the saints, ascended up before God out of the angel's hand. And the angel took the censer, and filled it with fire of the altar, and cast it into the earth: and there were voices, and thunderings, and lightnings, and an earthquake.
The Revelation of St John the Divine, 'The Seventh Seal'.

Incense Everywhere

Incense is a resinous gum given off by certain *boswellia* in India and Africa, and has a highly symbolic meaning. Since Antiquity, man has used it for religious ceremonies. The Egyptians, Persians, Greeks, Romans and others employed it at rites honouring their gods, for sacrifices and funerals. Christianity only adopted it in the 4th century, after it was admitted to the Empire of Constantine I the Great. As Hans Biedermann explains, 'The smoke of incense rising up to the sky was seen as a symbol of the way followed by the soul as it returned to its resting place, or prayers rising from the assembled faithful.' When blessed, incense plays the role of purifier. In this sense, its perfume was for a long time contrasted with the sulphurous odour of Satan.

Other Fumigations

Comparable symbolic attributions can be found in other civilisations. In Central America, the Maya used copal, a yellow resin from the copal tree which they called the 'brain of heaven'.

Arabian incense comes from a kind of juniper. In the Far East they use sandal, a lignous substance drawn from a parasitical plant from the tropical regions which, when burned, gives off a purifying smoke. But the incense known as 'Indian' is also widespread there. Buddhists use it for meditation, and every temple must have a supply of it.

A Biblical Perfume

When Baudelaire considered perfumes 'having the effusiveness of infinite things', he mentions incense, and also benzoin, a resin produced by trees of the genus *Styrax*. However, he does not include myrrh which, like benzoin, is mixed in incense – and more often than the latter. This resinous gum drawn from a tropical tree, the balsam or the cypress spurge, has a mythical source. When Myrrha, the mother of Adonis, fled from the wrath of her father, she reached Arabia, where the gods transformed her into a tree bearing myrrh. However, its symbolic importance results from its role in the New Testament. Along with gold and incense, it was one of the presents given by the Magi to the Infant Jesus. Then at Golgotha, before Jesus was crucified, the soldiers wanted to give him 'wine mixed with myrrh', which he refused. Later, Nicodemus provided a mixture of myrrh and aloes to prepare the body of Jesus, together with Joseph of Arimathea, before it was placed in the tomb.

Jan de Beer, *Adoration of the Magi*, 16th century. Musée de la Renaissance, Ecouen. '...the incense honours his divinity [that of Jesus] and the myrrh his humanity and burial, because this was the perfume used for burying the dead.' (Bossuet)

Papyrus censer from Lower Egypt, Saitic period. Musée du Louvre, Paris.

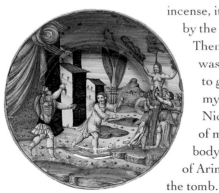

Left: Italian majolica from Urbino telling the story of Myrrha, 16th century. Musée de la Renaissance, Ecouen.

Appendices

❖

Practical Notes

THE SYMBOLISM OF NAMES

Chateaubriand wrote: 'The flower gives honey; it is the daughter of the morning, the charm of springtime, the source of perfumes, the gracefulness of virgins, the love of poets; it passes quickly, like man; but it gently yields up its flowers to the earth. Among the Ancients, it crowns the banquet cup and the white hair of the sage; the first Christians covered martyrs with it and the altar of catacombs; today, in memory of these ancient days, we place it in our temples.'

Although the flower is a symbol and conveys its message by rites that man has associated with it, it is also the vehicle for another, more accessible symbolic meaning by virtue of its name. Names are not given as a result of arbitrary choices. Perhaps the flowering pattern or the leaves recall some other form, or the name alludes to history or a legend linked to the flower, or it has a beneficial or evil effect. Names focus on the predominant aspect of the plant and are often rich in poetry.

FLOWERS OF LOVE

• The rose is the flower most intimately associated with love, and the names of certain

varieties reflect this. Red roses stand for ardent love, and what better names could there be than '**Dame de Coeur**' for a striking Hybrid Tea, or '**Lilli Marleen**' for a scarlet Floribunda?

• A gift of pink roses signifies a pledge of love, and the '**Prima Ballerina**', a cherry-pink Hybrid Tea, was perhaps named by some dreaming horticulturalist, struck by the theatrical allure of this flower.

• If a rose has yellow in it, admirers should beware, for this, in a rose, is the colour of infidelity. When red and yellow are mixed, they may be inclined to waver, but the miniature red-and-yellow '**Little Flirt**' was not so named for nothing.

• The pains of rejected or bygone love are aptly expressed in the drooping, catkin-like red-purple flowers of **Love-lies-bleeding** (*Amaranthus caudatus*).

• **Love-in-idleness** is, by contrast, pale blue in colour. This is *Nigella damascena*, originally from the Orient, whose rosette of bracts surrounding the flower have attracted other popular names such as '**Venus hair**' and, by contrast, '**Capuchin's beard**'. According to legend, love-in-idleness was originally white, but was changed to purple by Cupid. This story was later repeated by Shakespeare in *A Midsummer Night's Dream*: 'Yet marked I where the bolt of Cupid fell:

It fell upon
a little western flower.
Before milk-white, now
purple with love's wound,
And maidens call it,
Love-in-idleness.'

EVOCATIVE NAMES

Because of the shape of its
corolla, the **antirrhinum** is
known in England as the **snapdragon**. This is an apt name,
because when a bee lands on
the lower part of the flower, it
opens like a mouth. In France,
this flower was called the '**calf's
head**' and the '**calf's face**',
before they settled in the 19th
century for '**wolf's face**'.

• The **horsetails** take their
name from the resemblance of
the plant's whorls of branches to
a horse's tail. Another, unrelated
waterweed, the **marestail**, is so
named for the same reason.

• There are several stories to
explain the naming of the **horse
chestnut**, but the most appeal-
ing is that supplied by John
Gerard in his *Herball* of 1597: '...
for that the people of the East
countries do with the fruit
thereof cure their horses of the
cough'.

• In England, the **aconite** is
called the **monkshood** and in
France **Minerva's cap** from the
shape of its flowers. The whole
plant is poisonous, and the
alternative French name, '**wolf-
killer**', refers to this.

• 'Wort' is a Medieval English
word for a root or plant. The **St
John's wort** has been credited
since Ancient times with the
power to chase away demons.
It takes its name from St John
the Baptist, and the best time to
pick the plant for demon-
hounding purposes is on St
John's Eve in England, or in
France at noon on the saint's
day (24 June).

LEGENDARY ORIGINS

Some of the herbaceous plants
which grow wild in our climate
date back centuries, even as far
as Antiquity.

• The **gentian** is so named,
as Dioscorides claims, because
the king of Illyria, Gentius, was
the first to use it for medicinal
ends.

• The **common alchemilla** is
generally known as the **Lady's
Mantle**, a name given to it by
the alchemists who for their

mysterious researches collected the dew that gathered
during the night in its cone-
shaped leaves. It was a sacred
plant among the Ancients
because of its therapeutic qualities, and has always been
used for treating wounds As
Nicholas Culpeper (1616–1654)
states in his *Herbal*, 'it is proper
for those wounds that have
inflammations, and is effectual
to stay bleedings, vomitings,
and fluxes of all sorts...'

• The benefits of the **artemisia**
are mostly concerned with
regulating the menstrual cycle.
The plant takes its name either
from Artemis, the chaste virgin
goddess and protector of
women, or Artemisia, wife of
the satrap of Caria, Mausolus,
because she made great use
of the plant in the
4th century BC.

Index of Flowers and Trees

*N.B. The flowers in bold type
are discussed in greater detail.*

Bibliography

Attwater, Donald, *The Penguin Dictionary of Saints*, Penguin Books, Harmondsworth, 2nd edition, 1983.

Brewer's Dictionary of Phrase & Fable, Millennium Edition revised by Adrian Room, Cassell, London, 2000.

Brosse, Jacques, *Mythologie des Arbres*, Librairie Plon, Paris, 1989.

ibid, *La Magie des Plantes*, new edition, Albin Michel, Paris, 1990.

Culpeper, Nicholas, *Culpeper's Complete Herbal* 17th century, reissued W. Foulsham & Co. Ltd, London.

Decaisne, Jh. & Naudin, Ch., *Manuel de l'Amateur des Jardins*, Librairie Firmin Didot, Paris, end 19th century.

Fitter, Richard; Fitter, Alastair and Blamey, Marjorie, *The Wild Flowers of Britain and Northern Europe*, Collins, London, 1974.

Fortune, Robert, *Three Years Wandering in the Northern Provinces of China*, London, 1847, republished by Editions Hoëbke, Paris, 1994.

ibid., *A Journey to the Tea Countries of China*, London, 1852, republished by Editions Hoëbke, Paris, 1992.

Graves, Robert, *The Greek Myths*, 2 vols, Penguin Books, Harmondsworth, 1955.

Hall, James, *Hall's Dictionary of Subjects and Symbols in Art*, John Murray, London, 1974.

Herwig, Rob, *Your Flower Garden*, Mitchell Beazley, London, 1979.

Larousse Encyclopedia of Mythology, Hamlyn Group, London, new edition 1968.

Pelt, Jean-Marie, *Drogues et Plantes Magiques*, Horizons de France, Paris, 1971.

Robbins, Russell Hope, *The Encyclopedia of Witchcraft and Demonology*, Spring Books, London, 4th impression 1967.

Thacker, Robert *The History of Gardens*, Berkeley, California, 1979.

Various periodicals from the 19th and early 20th centuries.

Photographic Credits

Key to Abbreviations: t = top; c = centre; b = bottom; bg = background; l = left; r = right; tl = top left; tr = top right; bl = bottom left; br = bottom right.

Editor: Laurence Basset
Editorial secretary: Camille de Cacqueray
Designer: Sabine Houplain, assisted by Amaëlle Génot
Illustrations: Rougui Barry-Oger
Layout: Karin Crona

First published by Editions du Chêne, an imprint of Hachette-Livre
43 Quai de Grenelle, Paris 75905, Cedex 15, France
Under the title *Les Plantes et leurs symbols*
© 2000, Editions du Chêne – Hachette Livre
All rights reserved

Language translation produced by Translate-A-Book, Oxford

This edition published by Hachette Illustrated UK, Octopus Publishing Group,
2–4 Heron Quays, London E14 4JP
English Translation © 2004, Octopus Publishing Group, London

Printed in Singapore by Tien Wah Press
ISBN 1-84430-060-9